No Ordinary Man

Judge Forbes and His Library

Forbes Library 1894 - 1994

Allison McCrillis Lockwood

Dedication

For
Judge Charles Edward Forbes
and the staff —
past, present and future —
of the
Forbes Library

Contents

Acknowledgments

Many people have helped to make this book a reality, beginning with: Russell Carrier, President of the Board of Trustees of Forbes Library, who asked me to write it; Peter DeRose, co-publisher of the *Daily Hampshire Gazette* who agreed to publish it; and author-journalist-editor Richard Garvey, my husband, who faithfully read each chapter as I completed it.

The Forbes Library staff was with me all the way. Director Blaise Bisaillon and Head Reference Librarian Elise Bernier-Feeley steered me to vital material as did Becky Plimpton, library assistant and archival intern, whose index to Judge Forbes' journal, and eager interest in the project, proved a godsend. Reference librarian Elise Dennis also was of help. Art and Music Librarian Faith Kaufman and her assistant Brian Tabor were most helpful concerning historic photos. Alexce Douville, Automation Librarian and Cataloguer, and her staffers Paula Elliot and Kathy Mizula eagerly introduced me to what remains today of Judge Forbes' onetime personal library.

Others who lent assistance were: Lynne Bassette, Curator of Historic Northampton; Jim Bridgman of Northampton High School; Diana Carter, Administrative Secretary, First Churches of Northampton; Christina Cavalleri; David Leonard, Curator of Historical Society of Greenfield; Christine Skorupski, City Clerk of Northampton; and Margery Sly, Smith College Archivist.

The visual aspect of the book is due to the talent of graphics-designer Florence DeRose. John Hentz is responsible for the computer graphics on the cover. Gordon Daniels, Jennifer Burdick-Poitras and Jerrey Roberts, all on the *Gazette* staff, did the photography involved. Patricia Luchini incorporated the manuscript into the *Gazette* system. Receptionist Nancy Rhoades served as our "message center."

Guardian Angel of this book has been Philippa Stromgren, assistant to the publishers of the *Gazette,* and also promotion coordinator. "Pip" kept all of our efforts on line and ever moving forward. Her dedication, energy and enthusiasm inspired us all, — and especially myself.

Allison McCrillis Lockwood
Northampton, Massachusetts
August, 1994

Preface

The Forbes Library Centennial Committee, which I am privileged to cochair with Trustee Jan Hemminger, planned a year-long celebration to precede the 100th anniversary of the opening of the library on October 23, 1894.

Attendance at the many and varied activities indicates that residents of Northampton and others appreciate the unique philanthropy of Judge Charles Edward Forbes.

The judge listed in his daybook only one item which he wished to be in the library, should it ever be established. That was his favorite clock in his remarkable collection. That clock is being repaired and restored, and will begin on October 23, 1994, recording the time of the library's second century.

However, there is an even more permanent memorial to the judge and the remarkable library he founded. You are holding it in your hands.

When Trustee Chairman Russell Carrier read Allison Lockwood's "Touched With Fire, An American Community in World War II," he asked her to give Judge Forbes and his library the benefits of such careful research and such gifted presentation.

The Forbes Library Centennial committee is grateful that Allison Lockwood has given permanence to our celebration and has honored Judge Forbes with the one thing he valued even more than a fine timepiece — a good book.

Richard Garvey
Northampton Massachusetts
August, 1994

Introduction

One winter afternoon in 1926, my mother met me after class at the Vernon Street School where I was then in first grade. Down Elm Street we walked to the Forbes Library where she introduced me to the children's room up on the second floor. I remember the strange echo as we crossed the rubber rug in the lobby and also the book she drew to read to me, — "The Happy Prince and Other Stories" by Oscar Wilde. For the next seventeen years, until 1943, when I graduated from Smith College and went off to WWII, the library would be my second home.

My happiest memories of the Forbes involve the years of my adolescence coinciding with the Great Depression. A born bookworm, with a love of history both ancient and modern, I read my way through the storm and stress of the 1930s. Old, bent and bespectacled, my literary guide was Miss Annie Carlisle who, I now know, spent forty-seven years (1899-1946) of her life behind the loan desk. How delighted I was to discover her — young and smiling — in the middle of the front row in the first group photo of the original library staff taken around 1900. On learning I had seen the film *A Tale of Two Cities* at the Calvin, Miss Carlisle steered me to Thomas Carlisle's history of the French Revolution. When the first English translation of Hitler's *Mein Kampf* arrived at the Forbes in 1936, she herself handed it to this sixteen-year-old reader who had requested its purchase.

After more than four decades away from Northampton — during which time "my library" was the Library of Congress in Washington, D.C. — I came back to the Forbes in 1986. At the end of my first transaction with Reference Librarian Elise Bernier-Feeley, she smiled and said, "Welcome home."

Writing this book on the Forbes has thus been a labor of love. Besides considerable research, I spent many hours in the library, — watching, listening, asking questions, getting to know both staff and patrons. Based on the dedication, work ethic, courtesy, patience and fact I have observed on the part of the staff, I have concluded that the Forbes is the most civilized place in town or, as one patron remarked, "the best thing in Northampton."

One autumn Sunday afternoon at the Forbes, not long ago, stands out in my memory. The patrons appeared less charged and more relaxed than on a weekday, but it was nonetheless a busy period. I met patrons of every description: serious newspaper readers, lonely elders, students, unemployed young men, professionals seeking leisure reading, harried parents, idlers, and one young woman there simply to meet her boyfriend. All afternoon people came and went.

As closing time drew near, people were already drifting away. At five o'clock the old-fashioned gong was struck. Soon everyone was gone; the library was empty, dark and silent. For a moment or two I stood, lost in thought, amid the gathering gloom. The sound of a vacuum cleaner starting up in the Reference Room broke the stillness. And then the phone began to ring, — urgently, or so it seemed. It was still ringing as I went out the door. There on the steps stood a frustrated would-be patron who expressed his disappointment. "You'll have to come back tomorrow," I told him. "The library opens at nine."

Allison McCrillis Lockwood

Judge Charles E. Forbes

Chapter One

"A Munificent Bequest"

"**For some time Judge Forbes of this city has been in a failing condition and is now lying dangerously ill at his rooms in the Northampton National Bank building,**" reported the *Hampshire County Journal* — one of three weekly newspapers published in Northampton in the nineteenth century — to its readers on February 12, 1881.

Three days later, on February 15, the *Hampshire Gazette* and *Northampton Courier* announced the death of Judge Charles Edward Forbes who had died on the 13th "at about two o'clock on Sunday afternoon." Having thus, in turn, been scooped, as it were, because of different weekly publication dates, the *Journal* took pains in its own next edition on the 19th, to remind its readers that "the first intelligence" of Judge Forbes' illness had been "given to the public through the columns of *The Journal* last Friday."

For thirty years Northampton's "venerable jurist and learned

An 1870's view of Northampton's Main Street, as Judge Forbes would have seen it.

counsellor at law," as Forbes was described in an 1870s town directory, had occupied his two-room suite — "very commodious quarters" according to this same direc-

Forbes lived over the Northampton National Bank on the corner of Main and Center Street from 1851-1881. His rooms were on the top floor. The building (on right of photo) was modernized by William Fenno Pratt in 1870.

tory — over the Northampton National Bank building that still stands at the corner of Main and Center streets. It was in these quarters that the eighty-five year old judge died following a misadventure on a bitterly cold night a few days earlier.

Both the *Gazette* and *Journal* provided their readers with details of Judge Forbes' last illness and death. "It seems," reported the *Journal*, "that Mr. Forbes, who for a long time had been in poor health, was locked out of his rooms ... through his own mistake ... having misplaced the key to which he gained access to his room by a spring lock. It was a cold night, and he was lightly clad."

Some time during the night, the old man had apparently visited the lavatory out in the hallway and then found himself locked out of his warm living quarters. "About

two o'clock," reported the *Gazette*, "night-watchman William Partridge was attracted to the stairway leading to the Judge's apartments over the Northampton Bank, and on going to the top landing, found the Judge standing,

Deacon George Hubbard was a longtime friend of Forbes' and his executor. Together they wrote the will that in 1875 founded Smith College.

partly dressed and shivering in the cold, unconscious of his condition." Partridge assisted him back to his room, and the following morning, Deacon George Hubbard, a longtime friend and associate of Forbes, summoned Dr. James Dunlap, who had his office at 92 Main Street and, as nurse, a young man from Hartford, Edgar Carlisle.

For three days Judge Forbes lingered in an unconscious state and finally breathed his last on the afore-mentioned Sunday afternoon, February 13, 1881. The death certificate on file at City Hall lists his age as eighty-five years, five months, and nineteen days with cause of death listed as "congestion of the lungs" — apparently pneumonia.

"The funeral will take place from the Mansion House at three o'clock tomorrow afternoon," the *Gazette* advised its readers on February 14. And then, to remind them that the death of Charles Edward Forbes was more than just a routine mortuary event in the life of the town, the writer

added: "The Judge was a man of considerable property, $198,000 of his property having been taken from the Northampton National Bank at the time of the robbery in 1876. Of this, $128,000 was in registered U.S. bonds and $70,000 in railroad stocks. His estate is not unlikely to amount to a quarter of a million dollars."

"There has been," continued the *Gazette,* "much speculation as to what disposition the will makes of the property, but it is commonly considered that it is left for some object, or objects, of a public character to be carried out in this town."

The Mansion House, built in 1871, later known as the Fitch Hotel and in its last days as the Hotel Draper, was a handsome red-brick caravansary, with wrought-iron balconies, that then stood on the site of what is today 175 Main Street. It was there, at the Mansion House, only a few moment's walk from his home over the bank, that Judge Forbes had taken his meals in the hotel dining room and where

The Mansion House

FRANK KINGMAN, Proprietor.

129 Main St., - NORTHAMPTON, MASS.

he would long be remembered for his custom of tipping a certain waitress an extra fifty cents a month for making his toast to suit him each morning.

For an elderly bachelor who had literally spent most of his life on Main Street, and who had given up church-going some two decades earlier, the "parlors" of the Mansion House now seemed a suitable location for his funeral rites. "The funeral of Judge Forbes was well attended," reported the *Gazette*. "A large number of the Hampshire Bar, the professional and business men of the town, and some from out of town, were present." The *Journal* noted also the presence of "a number of ladies."

It is probably safe to assume that the undertaking services and the coffin were provided by one R.E. Edwards who, in the custom of this period, combined a coffin and furniture trade. Edwards was located close by at the rear of the First Church.

The funeral services were conducted by the Reverend William Leavitt of the First Church and the Reverend Charles Ferry of the Unitarian Society. Although he had given up church-going about 1860, Charles Forbes had nevertheless been a member of the First Church from the time of his arrival in Northampton in 1817 until 1825 when he and a distinguished group of dissidents left that church to form the Unitarian Society. In any event, these two ministers conducted the Forbes funeral: Ferry read the Sermon on the Mount and Leavitt "spoke in brief eulogy of the deceased," according to the *Journal*. Leavitt also "hinted at the nature of the will of the deceased by saying that the name of Charles Edward Forbes would go down to

Reverend William Solomon Leavitt, pastor of First Church, 1867-1881, delivered the eulogy at Forbes' funeral. He had an unusual connection with Forbes, who generally despised ministers and priests, but got to know Leavitt in his other role as librarian of the Clarke Library.

Dr. Thomas W. Meekins charged $20 to have his quartet sing at Forbes' funeral. A social leader who was involved in various musical groups, he was also Forbes' dentist.

posterity as one of the noblest of those who had benefited mankind.

"Music at the funeral," reported the *Gazette,* "was furnished by a quartette, under the direction of Dr. T.W. Meekins, who sang 'Remember Now Thy Creator' and 'Only Waiting.'" Thomas Meekins was a prominent dentist whose musical talents enlivened Northampton's social and cultural life in this period. "There were no floral decorations," observed the *Journal* reporter, "but there was a representation of a miniature sheaf of wheat, with a sickle beside it, lying on the coffin."

At the close of the funeral rites, Judge Forbes' remains were conveyed down Main Street and out to the Bridge Street Cemetery where, because of the frozen ground, actual burial would have to wait until spring. "After the remains were deposited in the tomb," the *Gazette* reported, "thirty or forty gentlemen gathered in the parlors in the Mansion House and listened to the reading of the Will of the deceased by Deacon George W. Hubbard, the surviving executor named in it. The reading was listened to with the closest attention." The will was described in the Journal as "a lengthy document, covering some fifteen pages of legal cap, in a very fine handwriting."

For news of the actual contents of Judge Forbes' will, ordinary citizens had to wait until Saturday, February 19th when the *Journal* came out with a special "EXTRA EDITION" to allay "the disappointment expressed because our regular edition of the *Journal* today did not contain the full text of the will of the late Judge Forbes." They boasted of the "extra expense" including "paper of extra quality" so that "citizens may preserve a copy in a convenient form."

This special edition began: "THE WILL! ... A MUNIFICENT BEQUEST TO NORTHAMPTON. For the Purpose of Founding a Public Library." Referring to the will as "this somewhat curious testament," the writer added that "the general curiosity is quite unusual, though excusable in view of its importance." This was followed by a quote from Shakespeare's Julius

LAST WILL AND TESTAMENT

OF

CHARLES E. FORBES,

LATE OF

NORTHAMPTON, MASS.

In response to the great surge of public interest, both the *Journal* and the *Gazette* published Forbes' will in its entirety.

Caesar: "The will! the will! the testament! You shall read us Caesar's will!" This lead ends with, "Well here's the Will of most interest to Northampton people." The will was then printed out in its entirety as it would be by the *Gazette* as well on its next publication date, three days later on February 22. The *Gazette* also provided extra copies "at the *Gazette* office, or at the news office."

LAST WILL AND TESTAMENT OF CHARLES E. FORBES, LATE OF NORTHAMPTON, MASS.

I CHARLES E. FORBES, of Northampton, in the county of Hampshire and Commonwealth of Massachusetts, being of sound and disposing mind and memory, do hereby make, publish and declare the following holograph to be my last will and testament, hereby revoking all wills and testaments by me at any time heretofore made.

1. I direct all my just debts and funeral expenses to be paid out of my estate by my executors hereinafter mentioned, together with the cost of a lot of ground and a decent monument to my memory, to be erected by them in the Cemetery in said Northampton.

2. I hereby give and devise to my half brother, Henry, of Enfield, in said county, an annuity of one thousand dollars a year during the period of his natural life.

Also my gold watch by Jules Jurgensen, and my gold watch vest chain with a hook in the form of a serpent's head at one end thereof.

3. I give, devise and bequeath to my sister Elizabeth, usually called Betsey, of said Enfield, an annuity of one thousand dollars a year during the period of her natural life, also my gold watch, a duplex repeater by Cooper, and my lightest gold watch neck chain, also all my beds, bedding, iron bedstead and furniture in my sleeping room together with my Wilson Adjustable Chair, now in my office.

It is my desire that the above annuities should be paid in quarterly payments as nearly as conveniently may be, on the first days of February, May, August and November in each year.

4. I give and bequeath to Charles F. Warner, who bears my name, in addition to what I have already given him, all my gold studs, gold sleeve buttons and silver studs, and buttons, fowling piece, London pistols and all my revolvers, ammunition and hunting apparatus of all descriptions.

Charles Forbes Warner. As a young boy he knew Forbes who gave him a $250 gold watch when he left Northampton at age 14, to learn the printing trade. He later returned to work as a newspaper editor and publisher.

5. I give and bequeath to the Second Congregational Society in said Northampton my pew in the Meeting House of said Society.

6. I hereby constitute and appoint the Hon. Samuel T. Spaulding, and the Hon. George W. Hubbard, both of said Northampton, to be the executors of this my last will and testament, and also to be the trustees of all the estate, goods, effects and property hereinafter given in trust by the same. It is my request to the Judge of Probate that no bonds with sureties be required, of said trustees, unless from a change of circumstances or for other sufficient reason he shall become satisfied that the safety of the trust funds is endangered by the omission, in which case he is requested to require bonds with adequate sureties, or to remove the delinquent trustee or trustees and to appoint other trustee or trustees in their stead.

Judge Samuel T. Spaulding, Forbes' partner for nine years between 1856 and 1865, was the co-executor of the judge's will.

7. I give and devise to said Spaulding the use of my Law Library so long as he shall remain in the practice of the legal profession.

And I recommend that a catalogue of the books composing the library be made out and lodged in the Probate office.

And I further give to the said Spaulding in the expectation that he will accept the above named office, and execute the above named trusts, my gold watch by the Waltham Company, a stem winder, and the case thereto belonging, also my heaviest gold watch neck chain.

8. I give and devise to the said Hubbard in like expectation, my gold pocket chronometer by Hutton, and the cases thereto belonging, also my gold vest watch chain with a large loop at the end thereof.

9. All the rest, residue and remainder of my property and estate, real, personal and mixed, wherever situate or of whatever the same may consist, I give, devise and bequeath to them, the said Spaulding and Hubbard, their heirs, executors, administrators and assigns, and to the heirs, executors, administrators and assigns of the survivor of them, and to such person as may be appointed trustee in the place and stead of either of them, and to his heirs, executors and administrators and assigns, but in trust nevertheless and for the uses and purposes hereinafter set forth, that is to say, to establish a fund of not less than two hundred and twenty thousand dollars ($220,000) in gold or the equivalent of gold in value, for the purchase of a site

and the erection of a building, or the purchase of a building for the accommodation of a Public Library, and for the purchase of books, &c., to be placed therein for the use of the Inhabitants of said town of Northampton and their successors forever.

And I hereby order and direct that in case it shall be here-after ascertained that by reason of heavy losses already sustained or that may be hereafter sustained, in consequence of unfortunate investments or other causes, my estate shall not be found sufficient to establish said fund of two hundred and twenty thousand dollars, after payment of debts, legacies and the expenses of administration, then and in that event my said trustees shall keep said residue and remainder safely and securely invested until the same, together with the accumulated income and interest, shall amount to said sum, and thereupon they shall divide the same into three separate parts or portions, that is to say:

A BUILDING FUND of fifty thousand dollars.

AN AID FUND of twenty thousand dollars

AND A BOOK FUND OF at least one hundred and fifty thousand dollars.

BUILDING FUND.

This fund is appropriated to the purchase of a suitable building, or to the purchase of a site and the erection thereon of a suitable building, for the reception and safe preservation of the contents of the Library. The building to be fire proof, and situate as centrally and as near the present Court House in said Northampton as circumstances will permit, and so

The first opera house in Northampton was in the big building on the corner of Main and Old South Street, across from where Forbes lived.

disconnected from all other buildings as not to be endangered by fire originating in them.

In the event of a division of the town, the building, library, and all the property, funds and endowments thereto belonging are to be held for the use of the town in which the present site of the Court House is located.

Should it be found that the above building fund of fifty thousand dollars is inadequate, I hereby authorize my said trustees, being thereto first directed by a vote of the town, to permit the whole sum of two hundred and twenty thousand dollars or upwards, to accumulate for a term not exceeding ten years, the income and accumulations from said sum to be then divided into equal moieties, one moiety to be added to the Building Fund, and the other moiety to be added to the Book Fund, and to constitute a part of that fund forever. All purchases of real estate under this Will to be evidenced by deed or deeds conveying a fee simple to said trustees, their heirs and assigns, in legal form, duly acknowledged and recorded, but in trust alway and for the trusts and uses indicated in this Will.

AID FUND.

This fund of twenty thousand dollars is to be securely invested and so kept invested forever. The income thereof is to be used in aid of the town in the payment of employes in and about the library, and in the payment for fuel, lights and other necessary expenses, to be therein incurred. With prudent management and for a time after the library is opened and while the number of books is small, the income from this fund ought to be sufficient to meet the current expenses. With the lapse of time the condition of affairs will change, but with due care, perserverance and a moderately liberal spirit, no reason is perceived why in the end this should not become an institution of great value to the town.

BOOK FUND

This fund is to consist, at the least, of one hundred and fifty thousand dollars, and in addition thereto of the balance, if any, of my estate, after deducting the building fund, the aid fund, and the book fund, all debts, legacies and the expenses of administration, and also in addition thereto of the moiety of the accumulations above mentioned, yielding annually the sum of nine thousand dollars, at the least, in gold of the present standard of the gold coinage of the United States or the equivalent thereof. This fund is to be securely invested in some productive property and to be kept so invested forever.

In making investments preference is to be given

1st. To first mortgages on real estate held in fee simple, under undoubted titles, to an amount not exceeding one half the value thereof in gold, exclusive of all buildings thereon.

2nd. To registered bonds of the United States.

3rd. To registered bonds of any one of the New England states or of the state of New York.

4th. To registered bonds of any city, County or town in New England, against which an action may be sustained at law to enforce its promises, and execution against which may be levied upon the person or estate of any inhabitant thereof.

5th. Beyond the above circle of investments, loans may be made upon such security as the inhabitants of the town, in legal town meeting, by a majority of ten to one, may order and direct, no loan, however, shall be made to any private individual or individuals, corporation or corporations unless secured by a mortgage or mortgages on real estate as is above required.

As this fund will be the mainspring of the institution, I will and direct, that in case of losses by reason of bad investments, dishonesty of treasurers, trustees or other officers, or from any other cause, whatever, the income arising from this fund and also from the Aid Fund shall be applied towards the making good of such losses and to no other purpose, until such losses are fully repaired.

The income from the Book fund, except as above directed, shall be applied exclusively to the purchase and repair of books, pamphlets, manuscripts and papers of a literary or scientific character, and the binding of the same. Maps and charts, and to a limited extent, statuary, paintings, engravings and photographs, may be purchased as ornaments to the library and aids to scientific inquiry. Said income shall never, under any pretence whatever, be directly or indirectly applied to any other use or purpose. It is not my intention, however, that the whole income should be expended each year, but the whole or such parts thereof as may be considered to be judicious under the circumstances then existing.

It is my design to form a library of works of science and the arts, in their broadest acceptation, of ancient and modern history, and of the literatures of our own and other nations; but as theological works cannot be wholly excluded, in the selection of these latter works no preference shall be given to any sect or system of theologic inquiry, but strict impartiality is to be extended to all of them. Histories of different religions may find an appropriate place in this department.

It has been asserted that there are between two and three thousand different systems of religion in existence. But as a general rule these are the inventions of cunning men or the vagaries of semi-lunatics, speaking boldly and impudently in the name of God, of whose decrees and purposes they know as little as the most ignorant of their victims. The result is seldom doubtful. It is wealth and power on the part of the prophets, ignorance and poverty on the part of the disciples.

It has been my aim to place within reach of the inhabitants of a town, in which I have lived long and pleasantly, the means of learning, if they are disposed to learn, the marvellous development of modern thought, and to enable them to judge of the destiny of the race on scientific evidence, rather than on metaphysical evidence alone. The importance of the education of the people cannot be overrated. It will be found the most efficient if not the only protection against the inroads of a foreign superstition, whose swarms of priests, Jesuits, monks, ministers and agents are let loose upon us, and engaged in the unholy work of enslav-

On May 22, 1876, P. T. Barnum's Circus paraded down Northampton's Main Street. Forbes made no mention of this in his journal.

ing the minds of the multitude, and moulding them into instruments of priestly power, a power built up on the remains of ancient paganism, and sustained in one particular at least by gross fetichism, a power growing out of a monstrous perversion of the precepts and example of the Founder of Christianity, by which poverty, lowliness, and self abnegation are forced to mean worldly grandeur, enormous wealth, a palace, absolutism and an earthly crown, as the contrast, so the antagonism must always remain, between enlightened freemen and the progeny of the Purple and Scarlet clad Mother. Let it be deeply engraven in the mind, that no strictly Roman Catholic country ever was, or ever can be, a free country.

I further will and direct that none but laymen shall be competent to any employment, or fill any office, or exercise any control in the management of the library.

From time to time rules and regulations will, of course, be adopted for the preservation and use of the library.

For the violation of such rules, in addition to legal remedies, the use of the library may be withheld from any inhabitant of the town either for a limited period, or for life. Any inhabitant of the town, having a right to the use of the library may request the trustee or trustees to be hereinafter chosen to place therein any book or work described in writing, and should the trustee or trustees decline to comply with such request, he or they shall state in writing the reasons therefor, which reasons shall be copied in full in the records of the library in order that the rights of the parties, if desired, may be determined at law.

The above bequest for the benefit of the Inhabitants of said Northampton is made on the following conditions:

1. That the town by vote shall accept said bequest within three years after the Probate of this will, and further

2. By a vote duly recorded and legally binding, the inhabitants of said town in their corporate capacity as a town shall obligate themselves and their successors.

1. To pay all expenses necessarily incurred in or about the management and administration of the affairs of said library over and above the income derived from the Aid Fund.

2. To keep the library building in repair, and to rebuild the same in case of its destruction by fire or other casualty.

3. To erect or provide such other building or buildings as may hereafter become necessary in consequences of the enlargement of the library.

If said town of Northampton refuses or neglects for the period of three years from and after the probate of this will to perform the above named conditions on their part to be performed, and to assume the obligations above mentioned, then and in that event, I hereby revoke all bequests herein before made for the benefit of said town, and declare the same to be null, void and of none effect. And thereupon I give, devise and bequeath all the said rest, residue and remainder of my estate and all accumulations thereof, and all the additions thereto, to the President and Fellows of Harvard College in the town of Cambridge, County of Middlesex and Commonwealth aforesaid, to be safely invested in some productive property and to be so kept and invested as a separate fund forever. The income from said fund is to be applied, exclusively, to the support and encouragement of one or more Professors of commanding intellect and acquirements and of a natural aptitude for such pursuits, to be wholly devoted to original scientific investigation: or to the procurement of the aids, means and appliances necessary or useful in such investigation.

It being my object to give to scientists of prominent capacity, an opportunity to pursue their favorite investigations, without hindrance, (as far as is practicable,) from the ordinary cares and responsibilities of life.

Should the trustees nominated and appointed by this will, or their successors in said trust, upon due inquiry, made as expeditiously as can be conveniently done after my decease, become satisfied that a majority of the inhabitants of said town of Northampton are disposed to accept the above bequest upon the conditions thereto annexed, it is recommended that an act be obtained from the Legislature incorporating said library, and giving to the town in their corporate capacity the requisite power and authority, by vote or votes duly passed in legal town meeting and recorded among the records of said town, to adopt and execute the provisions of this will, and to perform all the conditions and to assume all the obligations therein mentioned, and to be forever bound to the performance thereof.

And further that such act be obtained previously to any action of the town upon the subject.

It is recommended that the act of Incorporation authorize said town, at any annual or special meeting of the inhabitants thereof, legally notified and warned, to elect one, or at their option, three trustees of the library and a secretary and treasurer of the corporation, and all other agents and employes therein, and to remove the same at their pleasure, to fix the compensation of each, to establish all necessary rules and regulations for the library, and generally to control all the affairs of the corporation. But in the absence of action on the part of the town, the trustee or a majority of the trustees so elected, being first duly sworn to a faithful discharge of the duties of their office, shall have the general superintendence and management of the affairs of the corporation, shall appoint the librarian and other employes in the library and fix the compensation of each, and shall have power to remove any of them for sufficient cause. They shall also have power to remove the treasurer whenever in their judgment the safety of the corporation funds requires his removal, and may appoint a treasurer *pro tempore* to continue in office until the town have opportunity to act upon the subject. They shall watch over the pecuniary interests of the trust, and shall direct the treasurer in writing as to the investments to be made; they shall examine and approve in writing all vouchers of payment made by the treasurer, shall direct the purchase by the treasurer of all books, works, and other articles for the library; they shall establish all necessary rules and regulations as to the use of the library and for the preservation of the books and other property belonging thereto, and generally, they shall have all the powers of the town, had the town chosen to exercise them, except the election of trustees and of the secretary and treasurer of the corporation. Annually, or oftener if the town shall so direct, the trustee or trustees shall make to the town a written statement of the condition of the library, and of any improvements, alterations or changes which may have occurred to them in the interest of the corporation, and after a careful examination and scrutiny of the report of the treasurer, they shall certify its correctness, or if disapproved, they shall point out particularly and distinctly the errors, mistakes, omissions or inaccuracies which it contains, so as to enable the town to act understandingly on any question arising therefrom.

The Secretary being first duly sworn as aforesaid, shall make a true and perfect record of the acts and doings of the trustee, trustees and treasurer and of all acts and doings binding on the corporation.

In case of a vacancy in the office or inability of the Secretary to discharge his duties, a Secretary *pro tempore* may be appointed and sworn by the trustee or trustees who shall continue in office until a successor is elected by the town.

The Treasurer, sworn as aforesaid, shall give bonds to the corporation in such sum as the town may appoint, or in the absence of such appointment in such sum as the Selectmen of the town shall direct with good

The south side of Main Street, across from the old Courthouse, in 1865.

and sufficient sureties to the satisfaction of said Selectmen for the faithful discharge of his duties as Treasurer, the principal and sureties, by the terms of the bond, to remain responsible so long as the treasurer shall continue to act in that capacity either with or without a re-election.

It shall be the duty of the treasurer to collect all moneys due to the corporation, from time to time, as the same may fall due, to make such investments thereof as the trustee or a majority of the trustees may direct in writing, to pay all debts and sums of money due from the corporations under their direction, to keep a just and true account of all moneys received by him and of all moneys paid by him with correct vouchers therefor, and to pay over to the corporation all sums of money due from him promptly at the termination of his treasurership, and to make, under oath, annually and oftener, if the town shall so direct, a detailed report to the town of all sums of money or other valuables received by him for the corporation, and all sums of money paid by him for the corporation, with dates and names of all persons from whom received or to whom paid. This report shall be delivered to the trustee or trustees for his or their examination seven days at least before the time of the town meeting to which the report is addressed. All the records, accounts and papers of the corporation or relating to the interest or business thereof shall at all reasonable times and with due precaution for their security, be open to the examinaiton of any inhabitant of the town having a right to the use of the library.

After the acceptance of this bequest by the town and the formation of the several funds as is above set forth, the trustees named in this will or their successors in said trust shall proceed to the purchase of a site and the erection of a building thereon, or shall purchase a building for the use of said library, and after the erection or purchase of such building, said trustees shall convey, assign, transfer and set over to the trustee or trustees legally elected by the Inhabitants of said town of Northampton all the estate, real, personal and mixed, of whatever description or wherever situate so held by them in trust as aforesaid, to have and to hold to the trustee or trustees so elected as aforesaid and their successors in said office, forever, upon the trusts and for the uses and purposes herein before mentioned and described in this will (Interlineations and erasures before signature.)

In witness whereof, I, the said CHARLES E. FORBES, have hereunto set my hand and seal this twenty-fifth day of September, in the year of our Lord one thousand eight hundred and seventy-six.

CHARLES E. FORBES. "Seal."

Signed, sealed, published and declared by the above named Charles E. Forbes to be his last will and testament, in the presence of us, who at his request, and in his presence, have hereunto subscribed our names as witnesses to the same.

OSCAR EDWARDS.

JAMES L. WARRINER.

JOHN WHITTELSEY.

JOHN PRINCE.

THOS. M. MEEKINS.

Chapter Two

"The Man Whom Northampton's Citizens Will One Day Delight to Honor"

S carely had the terms of the will of the late Judge Forbes been read and digested by the citizens of Northampton, when controversy broke out. Reported the *Gazette* on March 22: "The will of the late Judge Forbes has been the principal topic of discussion in this town and vicinity since it ... was made public. Those who do not like it should remember that the estate bequeathed was the property of the deceased, earned and accumulated by him during a long life of industry and economy, and that it is the right of every man to dispose of his own as he pleases. This, Judge Forbes has done; and we are free to say ... that he has disposed of his estate in a manner that will do an immense amount of good to this community. It will give the town a public library that will surpass all others in the country — outside of the great cities."

In addition to the understandable curiosity on the part of Northampton's citizens, there were three main reasons behind the sudden rush of concern over the terms of the Forbes will. The first of these reasons centered around the already existing Northampton Public Library, established in 1874 in Memorial Hall that had been built for that purpose, and also for a museum — both of these institutions intended to honor Northampton's eighty-eight Civil War dead whose names are inscribed on bronze tablets in the lobby that once led into the main floor library.

Soon after the publication of the will, there formed an articulate group of prominent citizens led by Christopher Clarke, nephew of the deceased John Clarke whose beneficence had been

Memorial Hall, home of the Northampton Public Library, 1874-1915, was built for that purpose and to honor the city's Civil War dead.

instrumental in founding both the Clarke School for the Deaf and the Northampton Public Library that came, inevitably, to be known as the Clarke Library. The first ques-

John Clarke, chief benefactor of the Northampton public Library, later called the Clarke Library.

tion raised, of course, was why Northampton would need two public libraries. This question would be answered, finally, only with the death of Christopher

Clarke in 1915.

The second concern, stemming from the will, involved the fledgling Smith College that had been founded in 1875 only six years before Judge Forbes' death. On the same day the will was published in the *Gazette,* there also appeared this small anonymous item in a column composed of commentary on the will: "Before the will of Judge Forbes was made public, it was intended that the next building erected on the college grounds should be for a library. Whether the same intention remains with the trustees is not known, but that the college will be greatly helped by the carrying out of the will there can be no doubt." In the six years after its founding in 1875, and the publication of the Forbes will, with its gift to Northampton of a public library, Smith College had built: College Hall (1875); Gateway (1875) as the President's dwelling; and Hatfield Hall (1879) for classrooms to supplement those in College Hall itself. Between 1878

In 1904, in honor of Northampton's quarter-millenial celebration, Smith College's administration building was festooned with white cheese cloth, magenta rosettes and laurel wreaths.

and 1881 the college had built — or acquired — five residential houses. The college library facilities, however, consisted of a single room in College Hall and the Clarke Library of Northampton down on Main Street.

Four years later, in 1885, L. Clark Seelye, the founding president of Smith College, in a letter to the *Northampton Daily Herald,* would claim that in a private conversation between Judge Forbes and himself, shortly after he arrived in Northampton to assume the presidency of the college, he had been "advised not to spend the limited funds of the college for a library" as "the interests of Smith College should be well cared for." In other words, the college that had relied for the past ten years primarily on the Clarke Library was now expecting to use the facilities of the new public library to be founded under the terms of the Forbes will. And this indeed they would do from the founding of the Forbes Library in 1894 until

1905 when a town-versus-gown controversy erupted that finally ended the relationship and resulted in the building of the college library, today called the Neilson Library, in 1909. Thus it was that, during the decade that the trustees of the Forbes will allowed the fund to accrue and also to plan the location, there would be a struggle

L. Clark Seelye, first president of Smith College (1875-1910), claimed that Forbes advised him "not to spend the limited funds of the college for a library."

John B. O'Donnell, an Irish immigrant who became a prominent lawyer, judge, and Northampton's first Irish-Catholic mayor, responded publically to the anti-Catholic tirade in Forbes' will.

18

between proponents of the Clarke Library and the president of Smith College — more of which later.

One particular section of the Forbes will, upon its publication, caused considerable commotion in this age of still-strong religious conviction as the nineteenth century was drawing to its close. This was Judge Forbes' provision that "none but laymen shall be competent to any employment, or fill any office, or exercise any control in the management of the library." It was not alone this exclusion of any and all clergy from the operation of the library that stunned readers, however, but also Judge Forbes' 159-word fulmination against the Roman Catholic Church. Obviously a deeply rooted prejudice in the mind of Judge Forbes himself, the modern reader has to remember that this view was widely held — and not always covertly either — by the still powerful Protestant establishment of his time.

Through decades of reading and study, Charles Forbes had freed himself — so he believed — from the shackles of sectarian religion of all persuasions. And now, through his dream of a great public library, he proposed to offer this gift of intellectual liberation to the citizens of Northampton. "It has been my aim to place within the reach of the Inhabitants of a town, in which I have lived long and pleasantly, the means of learning, if they are disposed to learn, the marvellous development of modern thought, and to enable them to judge of the destiny of the race on scientific evidence rather than on metaphysical evidence alone. The importance of the education of the people cannot be overrated." The key phrases, of course, are "modern thought" and "scientific evidence." This expression of Judge Forbes' vaulting ambition is expressed in the large bronze tablet that hangs today on the wall in back of the circulation desk at the Forbes Library.

Reactions to the anti-clerical provisions of the Forbes will were swift in coming — first from the vast and powerful Protestant public. An editorial from *The Worcester Spy* was re-printed in the *Gazette*. "An insult to the profession!" fumed an anonymous commentator. "His prejudice has excluded no other class from the official management of the trust created by his will ... . By what hallucination was he affected! What "malice did he harbor and for what cause!"

Here in Northampton itself, the Reverend J. Sturgis Pearce, rector of St. John's Church, mounted his pulpit to express his anger at Judge Forbes' "effort to establish and cultivate the spirit of inquiry ... at the same time ignoring the very class of men to whom the world is indebted for mental and moral progress. It is to the church, the influence of ministers, to religious institutions, that the world owes its advances in learning. It has remained for the so-called liberal spirit of this age to discover that those hitherto the friends of learning are in reality its enemies and henceforth to be considered as dangerous men."

Roman Catholic reaction was slower in coming, at least as reported by the press, and when it came — a few years later — their spokesman was John B. O'Donnell. An Irish immigrant, O'Donnell worked, as a boy, in

19

one of the Florence mills. Supperless after the long days' work, he educated himself at night school and, through his hard work and ambition, became a prominent lawyer in Northampton, the city's first Irish-American mayor, and, finally, a judge. "I consider Judge Forbes' attack upon religion and the clergy," opined O'Donnell, taking no side, "entirely out of place in an instrument of this kind, yet his views were his own and he was entitled to them. In his act, he nobly rose above his prejudices and gave this munificent gift to the people irrespective of race, color or creed."

There was one other ripple of reaction to the will — albeit a small one — a month after its publication. Suddenly there appeared in the *Gazette* a letter to the editor signed merely with the letter "D." This letter disclosed that in Forbes' first or original will, dated April 10, 1870, there had been the following provision: "that the committee of the Library

and the treasurer, each and all of them, shall always be of the male sex." This first will had, however, been stolen together with the contents of the Northampton National Bank's vault during the legendary bank robbery of 1876. Included were Charles Forbes' fortunately registered stocks and bonds and his original will. In the new will that he wrote that same year to replace the stolen one, he omitted his anti-female provision.

On the fourth of April, two months after Judge Forbes' death the *Gazette* reported the introduction of a bill in the Legislature: "An Act to Incorporate the Forbes Library in Northampton." The eight paragraphs of this bill (Chapter 232. Acts of 1881) were printed in full for local readers. Northampton was authorized to accept the will (Chapter 241. Acts of 1881). On April 27, the will was probated, and in the Town Meeting of May 31, 1881, Judge Forbes' magnificent bequest to Northampton was officially

William Gaylord was appointed a trustee in 1888, and oversaw the building of Forbes Library.

Oscar Edwards, a trustee of Forbes Library from 1881-1894, was the proprietor of O. Edwards & Co., dealers in drugs, paints, oils and groceries, at 100 Main Street, Northampton.

accepted. By this prompt action, Northamptonians surmounted Judge Forbes' tricky provision that if his gift, on his terms, was not accepted then the bequest would go to Harvard. Strangely no one seems to have complained that the town was being pressured in any way. At this point it was also decided, as proposed by Judge Forbes himself, to allow the funds to accumulate for ten years.

Appointed by the Probate Court, the trustees of the future Forbes Library were George W. Hubbard, Oscar Edwards and William Gaylord. At some time during that crucial month of April, 1881, these men must have realized that one day there might be wanted a portrait of Judge Forbes to grace the institution that would be given his name. Despite his position and prestige in Northampton, Forbes had never been photographed let alone limned by an artist. Doubtless this was due to the old Puritan-Yankee inhibition against portraits thought to be expressions of worldly vanity and perhaps even akin to those "graven images" warned against in Scripture. In any event, no known portrait of Forbes exists save that of a photo taken of him after death and lying in his coffin. This photo was quite likely made by Hardie and Schadee, "Artist Photographers", whose studio was just next door to the bank building where Forbes lived and died.

On the supposition that perhaps one day a bronze bust of Forbes might be wanted for the library, a local artist was also called in by the trustees to perform a special service. Thus occurred one of the stranger episodes — at least to the twentieth-century mind so unac-cepting of death — that followed Judge Forbes' demise. "The body of Judge Forbes was taken from the tomb last Thursday and buried in a brick-lined grave located on the main avenue of the Bridge Street Cemetery, not far from the Cherry Street entrance," reported the *Gazette* on April 26th. "Before the interment," the article contin-ued, "the casket was opened and a cast taken of the Judge's features from which a bust will be made sometime, though there is no defi-nite plan for anything of the kind at present."

The above-mentioned cast, or death mask was made by a local artist, Wales Hotchkiss, whose stu-dio was located in the Union Block at 38 Main Street. His advertisements in town directories of this period read: "Pictures of Deceased Persons Copied in Oil, Crayon or Ink." Wrapped in a cloth, this plaster cast of Judge Forbes' features rests today in a basket kept in the vault off the Director's office at the Forbes Library. Quite touching, the mask is the face of an old man worn down by age and illness. The face, nevertheless, is strong and hand-some with lean, classic features: a noble forehead, high cheekbones, an aquiline or Roman nose, and firmly chiseled chin. It would be used later in the painting of a con-trived and lifeless oil portrait of Forbes that hangs today in the Reference Room and also in the sculpting of the somber bronze bust that once greeted library patrons — front and center — as they entered the library.

The artist who painted Judge Forbes' portrait doubtless suc-ceeded as well as could be expect-ed, given the circumstances under

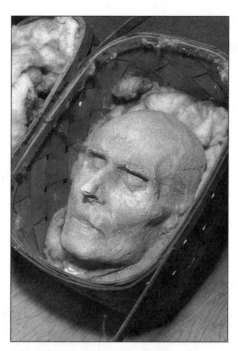

Two months after Forbes' death, his coffin was reopened and a plaster cast made of his features. This same "death mask" today rests in a basket in the vault at Forbes Library.

which she worked. "There has been placed on the wall of the reference room an oil portrait of the Founder of the library, Honorable Charles Edward Forbes, painted by Mrs. Louis Bradbury of Winchester," reported Librarian William P. Cutter in the Annual Report for 1907. "Although Judge Forbes refused during his lifetime to have a likeness made in any

Forbes, who refused to be photographed during his lifetime, was finally captured on camera in his coffin.

form, and no such likeness can be found, the artist has succeeded with the help of a death mask and descriptions obtained from those who knew him in life, in painting a portrait which is conceded to be as near a perfect likeness as could be prepared at this distant date."

In his 1914 Annual Report, Librarian Joseph Harrison would record "the placing of a bronze bust of Judge Forbes ... in the main entrance hall of the library." The sculptor was Bela Lyon Pratt of Boston, and the bust — about two feet in height — is slightly larger than life-size. It stands on a pedestal of Green Vermont marble and bears only the single word "Founder." Despite these two major efforts to preserve likenesses of Judge Forbes, there exists a third more modest effort that is possibly more appealing. This is a single pen-and-ink sketch that appeared on the front page of the *Gazette* for October 24, 1894, the day on which were reported the details of the library's formal dedication the previous evening. The sketch is so obviously based on the photo of Judge Forbes in his coffin that one suspects this is the work of the artist, Hotchkiss, who not only prepared death masks of "deceased persons" but also did "pictures in oil, crayon or ink." In any event, the simple pen-and-ink sketch that appeared in the *Gazette* is actually more lifelike than the three other renderings available to us of Judge Forbes' physical presence.

Once Forbes had been laid to rest, and the contents of the will dissected and digested, his executors then faced the dreary task of disposing — at public auction — of such remaining possessions of the old man as had not been dispensed of

by the will. Having never married, Forbes had lived all his life in rented quarters with the last three decades spent in his afore-mentioned suite above the Northampton National Bank, beginning in 1851. The building had changed during his years of occupancy as, in 1866, the bank had hired Northampton's leading nineteenth-century architect, William Fenno Pratt, to enlarge the building at the rear, to add on a third story, and to design a modern front. During this renovation period, Forbes had taken refuge in the Mansion House up the street.

"When the Bank commenced their operations," Forbes confided to his journal, "the officers thought — or said — they would complete them in six weeks. These six weeks have expanded to nearly six months." Nevertheless, Forbes was pleased with the building's new and "very beautiful" front and his own luxurious,

A bronze bust of Judge Forbes which once greeted patrons as they entered the library, now stands in the Reading Room.

new top-floor suite. "The expense cannot be less than ten or twelve thousand dollars. I occupy the whole third floor. The building is heated by hot air from the cellar."

After Forbes' death, one of the earliest visitors to his apartment, or "rooms" as such quarters were called in the nineteenth century, was the prominent Northampton lawyer, Charles Delano, a long-time acquaintance of Forbes and himself now "the oldest living member of the bar of Hampshire County" — to use his own reference.

"To stroll inquisitively through his rooms since his death, as I have done, within a day or two," observed Delano a fortnight after Forbes' death, "is to have gained a new view of this many-sided and widely cultured man." Lawyer Delano noted Forbes' "well-stocked library, filled with English and French authors of all ages, his numerous encyclopedias and lexicons, his atlases, maps and charts, his great store of modern works on science and philosophy ... his old sun-dial, his clocks and watches ... his field and opera glasses, his carefully preserved flute, his fowling-piece and five pistols and revolvers, his half-dozen sets of dumb-bells of all weights and sizes, the cast-off medical appliances by which he kept his mortal machine so long in working order — all let in new light upon the man's chosen solitude."

Northampton National Bank's remodeled and "modernized" front facade, was the work of architect William Fenno Pratt. Forbes was pleased with the building's new look and with his own new suite on the top floor.

The cast-off "appliances" to which Delano referred certainly must have included two devices that Judge Forbes had purchased from a company in Boston known as "Dr. Dio Lewis" and concerning which he saved the advertising circulars and correspondence found today among his papers, preserved at the Forbes Library. The first device, called "Dr. Dio Lewis's SPIROMETER," promised "a complete means of enlarging and strengthening the pulmonary apparatus." If used daily for half a year, the circular promised that "the voice will be doubled and the respiration free and full."

The other device, called "THE PANGYMNASTIKON," was of German origin and marketed in the U.S. also by "Dr. Dio Lewis." In effect, this device was a small, portable gymnasium that could be "put up in any parlor, or sitting room, and removed in a minute, leaving nothing to mar the appearance of the apartment ... the variety of exercises is something wonderful! ... the most remarkable invention in the whole field of Physical Culture!" A receipt signed by one F. Scott, "per Dio Lewis", discloses that this workout device of Judge Forbes cost $15.00 and that the several sets of wooden dumb-bells, or barbells, that he also ordered, cost sixty cents each.

And now, in March of 1881, all these onetime possessions — save those set aside in the will — were to be disposed of. "The estate of Judge Forbes has been inventoried at $307,000." reported the *Gazette* on March 22nd. "This includes his libraries, — in law and miscellaneous — the latter valued at $1,000, though it must have cost him very much more than that." A week later the *Gazette* would report on "Judge Forbes' Estate — What the Inventory Shows."

At last, the primary beneficiaries of the Forbes will, the citizens of Northampton, would learn the extent of the estate and its constitution. "The value of the articles of Judge Forbes' personal estate, including furniture, clothing, watches and clocks amounts to a little over $1,000. His pew in the Unitarian Church is valued at $50; law library, $200; Massachusetts Reports, $174; miscellaneous library, $1,000; cash on hand, $358; J.W. and M.E. Warner's promissory note, $60; 13 shares of Bank of Commerce Stock, $1,820; 86 shares of Holyoke Water Power Co., $7,200; 400 shares of Delaware and Hudson Canal Co., $40,000; 300 Peoria and Rock Island Railroad, $24,000; 20 U.S. Government 6 percent currency bonds of $5,000, $125,000; U.S.

THE PANGYMNASTIKON
BY PROFESSOR SCHREBER.

Government 5 percent bonds of '81, at par, $26,000; U.S. Government 5 percent bonds of '81, at par, $24,000; U.S. Government 4 per cent (at par), $39,500; $44,240. Total $305,149.89. If these bonds and stocks had been inventoried at their market value, instead of their par value, the estate would amount to a considerably larger sum."

Three months later, near the end

of May, the long-awaited auction of Judge Forbes' personal effects was held. The complete inventory is preserved with his papers — a sad listing of the leftovers of a human life such as: boots, gloves, shawls, and shirts; sissors (sic), pensals (sic), boxes, steal (sic) pens, and 4 pairs spectals (sic); 5 magnifining (sic) and 3 field glasses; brooms, brushes and dusters; 4 canes, 3 umbrellas, and a mousetrap; 2 nightcaps, 1 sugar bole (sic), 1 tin lantern, and 4 bottles of gin. A small notebooks lists the items and purchasers at the auction. A "gold head cane" went to B.E. Cook for one dollar, a silk umbrella to J.C. Mather for $1.00; and a razor to Charles Delano for fifty cents.

"Quite a number of citizens came who bid on the different articles," reported the *Journal*, "probably as much because of their association with the town's great benefactor as for their intrinsic value. About twenty razors were bid in for thirty and forty cents each; a handsome dressing case, costing perhaps $8.00, went for $4.00 (the auction account says $3.75); and a Malacca cane for sixty cents; two large and valuable field glasses went for two and three dollars; other articles accord-

ingly. Among the curiosities were some ropes long enough to reach from the third story of the bank building, in which he lived, to the ground. To the ends of these ropes were attached stout irons, for fastenings, and it is supposed they were intended to be used, in case of emergency, as fire-escapes."

The question as to the disposal of Judge Forbes' personal, or "miscellaneous", library is answered in a *Journal* story for July 5, 1884. "Some 3,000 volumes which were left by Judge Forbes in his rooms over the Northampton National Bank," reported the *Journal*, "have been removed to more convenient quarters. These books will be the nucleus of the future Forbes Library. His law library was mostly disposed of by will, and a part of it is now owned by the county and is a part of the county law library."

A final mortuary

Judge Forbes' legendary unbrella was the topic of this sketch and a poem published in the Hampshire City Journal in 1887, and was later given to the library that bears his name.

event for the late Judge Forbes took place in the spring of 1882: the erection of "a decent monument", as provided for in the will, over his grave in the Bridge Street Cemetery. "The monument arrived Monday," reported the *Journal* on April 4. "It is of granite from Westerley, R.I. It stands upon a triple base, the first of which is six feet square and bearing upon its front in large, raised block letters, the name 'Forbes.' The next sub-base is of about the same thickness as the other, and of about a foot less square area than the main base. These two bases support a cube of almost four feet with polished surface and four half columns at the corners. On the front of this cube is the tablet bearing this inscription:

Charles E. Forbes
born
August 25, 1795
died
February 13, 1881
Founder of the Forbes Library

Above this cube-tablet, the shaft, about fifteen feet of obelisk form, tapers from two and a half to about one and a half feet at the top. J.C. Ritter of New Haven was the designer and said that the work occupied six months."

The reporter, who had made such close study of the new Forbes monument was annoyed that he could not include the cost in his report. "Everybody connected with the work seems to have a malicious sort of pleasure in keeping the cost of the monument from this reporter for some inscrutable reason. Whether the executors are afraid of being thought extrava-

gant, we don't know. That is not our opinion, certainly. Take it all in all," concluded the reporter, "the monument is a massive, substantial, and characteristic memorial to the man whom Northampton's citizens will one day delight to honor."

Forbes' "decent monument" over his grave in the Bridge Street Cemetery, as provided for in his will, shown here in a 1994 photograph.

Chapter Three

"To Him Pure Law Was the Perfection of Reason"

C

The great surge of public interest in the terms of Judge Forbes' will was accompanied by a sudden interest in details of the life of this man who, for the last twenty years, had lived an increasingly reclusive existence in his rooms over the bank at the corner of Main and Center Streets. Once he was gone, as a matter of fact, many Northamptonians were apparently remembering him only as aloof and withdrawn. In reality, Judge Forbes was a victim of his own longevity. For a man born in 1795, his life expectancy would have been about thirty-four-and-a-half years. He lived to be 85. Most of the prominent lawyers that Forbes had been associated with had, by the time of his own death, long since predeceased him: Jonathan Huntington Lyman (Forbes' first partner) at 42 in 1825; Isaac C. Bates at 65 in 1845; Rufus Choate at 60 in 1859; Charles Huntington (one of Forbes' partners) at 66 in 1868; George Ashmun at 65 in 1870; Osmyn Baker at 75 in 1875; and Samuel Spaulding (Forbes' last partner) at 58 in 1877.

Once active in the social, cultural, religious and political life of

Judge Forbes' Main Street neighborhood, where he walked, worked, dined and died. His funeral was held at the Mansion House, in the center of the block.

Northampton, Charles Forbes began — after closing his law practice in 1865 — to withdraw ever more into his own private world. Possibly, the crass post-Civil War boom years, now called "the gilded age," repelled him. Perhaps it was the vast changes in human life and expectations tak-ing place even in rural Northampton that alienated him. Between the year of his arrival here, 1817, and the year of his death, 1881, for example, the population of the town had quadrupled.

As the years passed, Judge Forbes acknowledged their passing with a tinge of sadness. To the end of his days he kept the brief and hurried letter from Enfield, in 1843, telling him his father was "dangerously sick." By the time this reached Northampton, his father had died, a fact he mourned in his journal. In 1861, when his sister Susan died — whom he had visited regularly in Enfield throughout her life — he wrote in his journal: "And what is life? It seems but an hour since we were children together ... and now we are rapidly passing away." On his own eighty-first birthday, August 25, 1876, he wrote: "Birthday. 81 years old, or 9 times 9, the grand climacteric, as some writers attest. My health is much better than it was a year ago. But I am not unaware of the end which soon awaits me." Four years later, he recorded his last birthday on August 25, 1880. "Birthday. 85 years

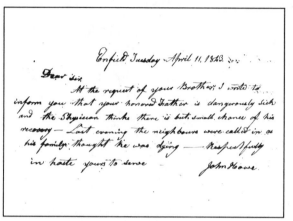

This brief letter from John Howe informed Forbes that his father was "dangerously sick." He died before it reached Northampton.

Forbes grew up in Enfield, Mass., one of the small towns now under the Quabbin Reservoir. Forbes left Enfield in 1817, but continued to visit his family there every year.

old. It will 65 years on Wednesday the first of next month since I was graduated. *Multa petentibus. Desunt multa. Bene ist, cui Deus obtulit. Parca, quod satis, manu.*"*

At some point during these last years, Forbes remarked to a friend: "The old are a burden to society. People care nothing for them, and that is why I keep within myself."

Now, in the late winter and early spring following his death, the onetime colleagues and old friends that survived him strove to recall and record the life of Charles Forbes particularly as he was in his prime. Most of these recollections were by members of the Hampshire County Bar who had known him; there were others such as his bookseller, Joseph Marsh. The rest of the life of Charles Edward Forbes is found — in his own fine handwriting — in the journal he kept from 1839 until his death. Even here, however, his innate reserve, dignity, self control and sense of decorum preclude — for the most part — anything resembling confession or revelation.

Of Judge Forbes' early years there is little known except that he was born on August 25, 1795, in that part of Bridgewater, Massachusetts known later as West Bridgewater. His family stemmed from old Puritan stock that had arrived in the new world in the seventeenth century. The family spelled the name "Fobes," but as an adult, and believing himself to be of Scottish origins, Charles would change the spelling of his name to "Forbes." Also, he would take the middle name of "Edward."

When Charles, the first-born, was one year of age, the family moved to Enfield, — today one of the lost towns lying under the Quabbin Reservoir. Here, his father, Jesse Fobes, a farmer, also played a role in politics, serving as Selectman for four terms and also in the Legislature from 1820-1822. Jesse Fobes and his second wife, Mary, produced eight children, three of whom died in infancy, another in middle age. The mother of this brood died when Charles was twelve.

At some point, like many New England youths of his era, Charles proposed to leave the farm, acquire an education and enter a profession. He was prepared for college by a local clergyman, another custom of that time, the Reverend Joshua Crosby of Enfield. Crosby was assisted by the Reverend Joseph Blodgett of Greenwich, who had attended Brown University and thus perhaps influenced young Forbes to apply to that institution where he was admitted in 1811 at age sixteen.

A charming first letter home to his father, dated October 19, 1811, survives. After briefly describing his journey, his room assignments, and his roommates, Charles tactfully expressed his need for more money after listing the purchases he had had to make. "Eight or ten dollars I need very much." Most of the letter, however, is a paean — couched in superlatives — to his new surroundings: "one of the most beautiful places that nature ever formed ... the most pleasant prospect, perhaps, in America. On

<hr>

To those who seek for much, much is ever lacking; blest is he to whom God with frugal hand has given just enough.
Hor. Car. Lit. III vol. 16

the South you behold the ocean ...
while on the East may be seen the
most delightful grove; on the West
a thriving town that wears all the
ornaments which are the offspring
of industry and wealth." He closes
with a rhetorical question that
raises the possibility of some
youthful illness or medical condition he has survived. "But what
the sight, what the view — without health — which although I
now enjoy, I know not how soon I
may be deprived of ... Your most

dutiful and affectionate son. Sic
vale, vale, care Pater." He would
graduate with the class of 1815.

After graduating from Brown,
young Forbes, who had decided to
enter the legal profession, began
to "read law," or study law — as
was then the custom — with an
established member of the bar.
Forbes began with Elihu Lyman,
in Enfield, but at some point
decided to seek his fortune in
Northampton, arriving here in
1817. Thanks to a small item in

ESTABLISHED IN 1786.

HAMPSHIRE GAZETTE!

Immediately after Forbes' father settled in Enfield, Mass. in 1796, he took out a subscription to the Hampshire Gazette, thus starting a family tradition that would continue unbroken for eighty-five years.

Best Advertising Medium

IN HAMPSHIRE COUNTY.

the *Gazette* at the time of his death, it is apparent that Northampton was not unknown to the Fobes family. "Immediately after the father of the late Judge Forbes settled in Enfield in 1796," reported the *Gazette,* "he subscribed for the *Hampshire Gazette* then delivered to subscribers in that town by a Mr. Hooker, postrider. He continued to take the paper as long as he lived, and his son, Deacon Henry Fobes of Enfield, has continued to take it ever since. Thus this paper has been in the family for eighty-five years." A second scrap of evidence, tucked away in a Forbes' journal entry in 1876, is the following reminiscence: "Forty-six years ago ... it was in the summer of that year, 1816, that I first saw Northampton." An earlier entry, concerning the death of an associate, indicates a business trip to Pelham in that same summer, so perhaps it was this occasion that had brought him to Northampton, — most likely to the courthouse of Hampshire County.

In any event, in 1817, young Forbes came to Northampton where he continued to read law, now with the Hon. Elijah Hunt Mills, a future United States Senator and a man for whom scrupulous Charles Forbes would always express high regard. In less than a year, Forbes himself was admitted to the Hampshire County Bar.

Soon after his admission to the bar, Forbes entered what appeared to be a promising partnership with one of the most respected lawyers in Northampton, Jonathan Huntington Lyman, a future chief Justice of the Court of Sessions, and also County Attorney. At

some point during their association, Forbes made what proved to be the grave mistake of co-signing notes for Lyman — twelve years his senior and presumed mentor in the law. Thus, at age twenty-five and starting to make his way in Northampton, Forbes found himself suddenly in debt — through no fault of his own save naivete — to the tune of $1,000. This was a considerable sum back then, comparable to forty times that figure today. This co-signing of Lyman's notes somehow also involved certain Southern students attending George Bancroft's Round Hill School, founded in 1823 and in operation until 1833. In his customary terse fashion, a few years before he died, Forbes confided to historian-journalist Henry M. Burt, whom he had

The Honorable Elijah Hunt Mills. In 1818, Forbes came to Northampton to read law with Mills, who later became a United States Senator. Forbes always expressed a high regard for him.

known when the latter was a print-ers-devil at the *Gazette* during his youth, the crushing burden of debt that Lyman had placed upon him. "He stated that during his partnership with Mr. Lyman he endorsed notes to him, and on his failure, he lost $1,000. Then, in addition to this, when the famous Round Hill school was in existence, he loaned money to some of the Southern students and lost heavily through them. In alluding to these misfortunes he said, 'These transactions taught me a lesson which I never forgot. I was greatly embarrassed by them, and it was not until 1832 that I got out of debt." He would then have been thirty-seven years of age.

During his sixty-four years here in Northampton, Forbes carefully recorded in his journal his series of rented accommodations. At the beginning, he boarded with Dr. Daniel Stebbins on Bridge Street, but for almost two decades, between 1822 and 1841, he lived in Pleasant Street at a genteel boarding establishment owned and operated by Mary Upham. When, in 1841, Miss Upham gave up her Northampton business to move to Cambridge to open another boarding house, Forbes recorded his move to the Mansion House, an earlier hostelry whose name was later adopted for a new hotel on Main Street. The old Mansion House sat on the hillside, now occupied by St. Mary's rectory, and overlooked the local dock of the New Haven and Northampton Canal that opened in 1835 and operated until 1847. This was an upscale move for young Forbes of whom, forty years later in an obituary, a friend would recall that "his practice warranted hotel board" by that time, rather than "a boarding house on Pleasant Street."

The two decades spent living at Miss Upham's did include however, so certain of his friends always maintained, an unsuccessful courtship and proposal of marriage to a woman never named. Was this one of Mary Upham's many transient as well as permanent boarders? Forbes did record some of these persons in his journal, for

The Red Castle, 67 King Street, Northampton, home of Jonathan Huntington Lyman, 1814. Shortly after his admission to the bar, Forbes became Lyman's law partner. The house was torn down in 1939.

The original Mansion House Hotel was on a hill (on the site now occupied by St. Mary's rectory) overlooking the dock of the New Haven and Northampton Canal.

example, a "Miss Goodwin of New York ... young and very intelligent," in July of 1839. Or could it possibly have been Mary Upham herself? There is a cryptic reference in the journal to his being "absent a few months in the summer of 1833, I think." In any event, he faithfully records Miss Upham's departure from Northampton in 1841. His next mention of her appears on March 9, 1859, eighteen years later. Apparently he had just received news of her death. "Miss Mary Upham died suddenly at Cambridge. She fell in the street and died immediately. Her age must be about 65 yrs. One of the best and most intelligent women I have ever known. I was a boarder in the family nearly twenty years until they moved to Cambridge in 1841.

At this point in his life, 1859, Forbes himself was age sixty-four which means that during his years under Mary Upham's roof, they were contemporaries, aged twenty-five to forty-five. Merely "an ordinary boy's affair" is how one Forbes associate would later refer to the alleged disappointment-in-

love of our subject. True or not, Charles Forbes remained unmarried to the end of his life.

The thirty years that followed his admission to the bar in 1818 were the most active of Forbes' legal career. After his unfortunate experience as Lyman's partner, he struck out on his own, — combining legal work with politics. In 1825 and again in 1826, he was elected to the General Court, or state legislature. He was appointed Chairman of the Highway Commission in 1836 and County Attorney that same year. As the latter, he would be remembered, after his death, by C. Parkman Judd, son of *Gazette* editor Sylvester Judd, a Boston attorney, as "very successful in prosecuting criminals. His indictments were noted for strict accuracy and the clear description of crime. His arguments to juries were clear, plain, crisp and forceful ... without wasting one idle word. When he indicted a man, conviction was sure to follow."

In 1834, life would deal the rising young lawyer Forbes a hard blow to his pride and ambition, one that was well documented at the time, and one that surely had a lasting effect on him. A vacancy occurred that year in the office of Judge of Probate, a position that Forbes greatly coveted, and he let this ambition be known. A petition on his behalf, bearing the signatures of members of the bar and prominent citizens of the county was forwarded to Governor Levi Lincoln recommending Forbes' appointment as Judge of Probate. Suddenly, he found himself up against Northampton's powerful religious establishment.

In 1825, together with about forty other distinguished parishioners, Charles Forbes had left the First Congregational Society, or First Church, and formed the Second Congregational Society, or Unitarian Church as it was later called. Forbes had participated in the dedication of the new Greek Revival edifice that stood on the same site the Unitarian Society occupies today, and even laid the cornerstone at that event.

"There was strong feeling about that time, in this section, that the Unitarians were getting into office too much," the *Journal* would observe, in 1881, following Forbes' death. "He was defeated by religious bigotry ... there was then a bitter prejudice against the Unitarian denomination, and Governor Lincoln appointed Judge Conkey instead. This concession to the religious bigotry at the time did much to embitter the mind of Judge Forbes and caused him to judge the religious world rather harshly perhaps."

Sylvester Judd, editor of the *Gazette* at the time this episode in Forbes' life was taking place in 1834, may have been one of those Northamptonians who defeated

him. In Judd's now famous manuscript he wrote: "Mr. Forbes is able and upright but cold, unfeeling and without sympathy for man, woman or child. Many of us would prefer Judge Conkey."

In 1835, Forbes was appointed Master of Chancery for the counties of Hampshire, Hampden and Franklin, and in 1835 and 1836 he served on the commission for codifying the Common Law. This involved the first revision and consolidation of the statues since the adoption of the constitution. Forbes wrote of this assignment: "My heart was in the work, and my labour was, I thought, of value to the public."

Over the next seven years, Forbes occupied himself with his own law practice, but in 1844 Governor George Briggs offered him the office of the Chief Justice of the Court of Common Pleas. For reasons known only to himself, he declined. Three years later, in 1847, Briggs urged Forbes to accept a commission as an associate justice on the bench of this same court, and he accepted. In later years, in a letter to Solomon Clark who compiled a book based on Northampton's university or college-educated business and professional men, Forbes confided that he had accepted the judgeship — in which he served only about six months, "not with the intention of remaining there permanently but as a graceful way of retiring from practice in the courts."

That same year, Forbes became a participant, as an attorney, in the Oliver Smith Will case. This involved the effort of disappointed would-be heirs and heiresses to contest the will of their kinsman, Oliver Smith, Hampshire County's

Charles P. Huntington was Forbes' third law partner. He was involved in the Oliver Smith will case.

The Hon. Rufus Choate, who was retained to challenge Oliver Smith's will on behalf of his would-be heirs.

Charles Delano, law partner to Osmyn Baker at the time of the Oliver Smith will case.

The Hon. Daniel Webster was hired to defend Oliver Smith's will.

Northampton attorney Osmyn Baker assisted Daniel Webster with the Oliver Smith will case, together with Charles Forbes.

first great philanthropist. The purpose of the will was to establish Smith Charities, the institution that for the past 152 years has helped widows with minor children and aided young men and women in learning useful trades and skills and even to provide modest dowries for brides.

Relinquishing their original plan of contending that Oliver Smith had been of unsound mind when he made his will, the frustrated would-be heirs instead sought to establish that one of the witnesses to the will, Theophilus Parsons

Phelps, was incompetent. Attorney Charles P. Huntington, a future partner of Forbes, was hired to prove this charge; the brilliant lawyer Rufus Choate, whose years in the U.S. Senate had won him wide acclaim, was also retained.

Six of the eight towns intended to be beneficiaries under the Oliver Smith Will accepted the challenge. Hired to defend the will was Daniel Webster, no less, with attorneys Osmyn Baker and Charles Forbes of Northampton to assist him. On July 6, 1847, the special hearing took place in the Hampshire County courthouse.

On his arrival in Northampton, Webster put up at the Mansion House, where Charles Forbes resided, and whose landlord circumvented his temperance rule so that Webster could enjoy his customary spirits. After Forbes' death in 1881, Attorney Charles Delano who, at the time, was a youthful partner of Osmyn Baker, recalled "the great consultation in Mr. Webster's rooms at

The Smith Charities building, at the exreme right, established through the Oliver Smith will, still stands on the same Main Street site, just below the corner of King Street.

the old Mansion House ... on the afternoon before the trial of the celebrated Oliver Smith Will case. There were present in that conclave, Daniel Webster, Osmyn Baker, Charles Forbes and my ardent but comparatively unprofitable self." Judge David Aiken, a future partner of Forbes and who outlived him by fourteen years, recalled not long before his death in 1895, that he too was present at "the great consultation" and that its purpose was "to load Webster up with facts concerning the case" and that it was Forbes who "made the statement of the case and clearly outlined the situation. Upon this and what he had gathered before, Webster made the

argument."

At the close of the conclave of three or four hours, Delano remembered that "as one of the results, two persons might have been seen moving towards Hadley at an unusual speed in an open buggy and drawing up at the house of Charles P. Phelps. The two missionaries on that occasion were Charles E. Forbes and the present reminiscent. The errand was a vital one," explained Delano, "no less than to *inspect the mind* of Theophilus Parsons Phelps, the vulnerable and doubtful witness to the will, a young man of solitary habits and marked temperament but of scholarly attainments, and the grandson of Massachusetts' great Chief Justice Parsons; and to endeavor by proper suggestions and persuasions to encourage the sensitive and timid witness, so that he might be prepared the next day boldly to take the witness stand and submit himself to the fearful ordeal of Mr. Choate's cross examination.

Lawyer Delano did not spell out the techniques used by Forbes, now a seasoned lawyer of fifty-two and himself, a relative twenty-seven-years-old fledgling in the law. Whatever tack they took, it worked. "The interview was attended with success," Delano boasted, "and the next day ... the hitherto reluctant and shrinking witness buoyed up by a masterly examination by the 'Great Expounder' (Webster) met the cross examination of the adversary with perfect composure and triumphant success. Messrs. Choate, Chapman and Huntington were baffled ... Phelps, Webster, Forbes and Baker were correspondingly delighted to see the mission to Hadley so happily vindicated." Webster was paid a retaining fee of $500 plus $1,000 for the argument while Baker and Forbes each received $250.

Forbes' own record of the Oliver Smith Will case, written at the time in his journal, is customarily terse: "Trial of the case of Oliver Smith's Will in the Supreme Judicial Court before Judge Wilde. Attys. Webster, Baker and myself for the will and Attys. Choate, Chapman and Huntington for the heirs. The will established by consent of the jury and no exceptions taken. Only one issue put to the jury, to wit the competence of Theophilus P. Phelps as an attesting witness. The question of sanity of the testator waived by the heirs." No self-congratulation here.

The following year, 1848, there came to Forbes the capstone of his legal career when he was offered an appointment by Governor Briggs as an associate justice of the Supreme Judicial Court. Forbes was appointed on February 8, 1848, and sat at Boston during the March term, at Lenox and Northampton during the September term, and for a short time in October at Worcester. "Received my commisson as a Justice of the Supreme Judicial Court, dated February 7, 1848," was Forbes' sole comment in his journal. This same year, he was awarded an honorary doctorate by his alma mater, Brown University. He preserved the letter from Dr. Francis Wayland, president of Brown, notifying him of his honor. It is among his papers at the Forbes Library.

After his death, a recollection of Judge Forbes in his prime as a SJC justice, was written for the *Gazette* by C. Parkman Judd: "Judge Forbes shone brightest in the Supreme Court. Here few were equal to him and none superior. In pure law he was a perfect master .... He worked very slow but always sure ... and gave full scope to his wonderful reasoning power; to him pure law was the perfection of reason ... the Court always gave the Judge the closest attention."

"The office sought him, not he the office," Judd believed. "He took the office with delight, and at first much pleasure. He held the scales of justice with an even hand. Cool and quiet, he never got excited or was disturbed. He gave his whole attention to the case on trial before him. He heard every word of evidence ... I can see him now, sitting on the bench, apparently as cold as an icicle, as unmoved as an iceberg, yet hearing every word and listening with full attention. He was prompt and clear in all his rulings ... in his charges to the jury the Judge was plain, clear, very fair and wholly impartial... .He held the court with the utmost dignity and decorum, ability and impartiality. Erect, manly ... he was universally respected by the bar, the jury and the public in attendance. Judge Forbes made one of the best judges ever on the bench of the S.J.C.

Suddenly, however, on October 7, 1848, only eight months after his appointment, Forbes resigned from the Court in "a manner most extra-ordinary" as Judd phrased it. The Court had been sitting all week at Worcester. Forbes was present all week through Friday, and then, "without saying a word to his associates, wrote and sent to the governor his resignation and then started for Northampton Saturday morning. The Court reassembled but delayed business until Judge Forbes should arrive. He never returned."

In his journal entry on the day of his resignation, Forbes recorded merely: "Returned from Worcester. Expenses $141.30. Resigned the office of a Justice of the Supreme Judicial Court." Three decades later, upon Forbes' death, Judd would write: "His associates were in a maze, for the night before they had all retired from the court room in perfect harmony: his friends were all puzzled ... there did not appear to be the slightest reason for the sudden step ... It is still a mystery today."

Near the end of his life, Forbes confided to Henry Burt," I held the commission, according to my present recollection, less than a year. I did not like it. The fact is, office looks quite differently to a man when he is dependent upon it for a living than it does when he is not." He found, he added, that "the work of a judge of the Supreme Judicial Court, at that time, was very hard. Unlike the present custom, opinions were written out *immediately*. A case might be argued on the first of the week and towards the close you might expect the opinion." Such haste would have been a sore trial to one as scrupulous, methodical and deliberate as Charles Forbes. These opinions apparently had to be written after hearing cases all day, followed by dinner and then discussion among the judges until about 9 p.m. Forbes had found himself writing until one o'clock the next morning.

"The air of the court rooms was always bad," Forbes also confided to Burt, nor did he enjoy the comfortless coach rides between towns and being "tossed from hotel to hotel" as he put it. The constant hurry also went against his grain. "Hurry up, Mr. Justice Forbes, or you will be late," Chief Justice Lemuel Shaw once remarked as the two men were, after their dinner, returning to the courthouse the bell of which was ringing. "I am tired of being tied to that bell," Forbes responded. His resignation followed not long after.

Judge Forbes settled back into life in Northampton and resumed his law practice but now, as he himself termed it, as a "Chamber lawyer." Many years later he would say: "Since I left the bench, I have attended court but two or three times — and then only as a witness."

In 1851, Forbes formed a partnership with Charles P. Huntington, one of the lawyers who had been on the opposing side in the Oliver Smith Will case. This partnership lasted until 1855 when Huntington was appointed a judge of the Superior Court. Upon his onetime partner's death in 1868, Forbes would write a long two-page history of Huntington's life in the journal ending as follows. "I thought of publishing in a newspaper of a sketch of Mr. Huntington's character, and indeed I commenced writing one. It occurred to me that unless I gave him credit for honor, truth, integrity and fair dealing in all things, it would be best to remain silent." These qualities, it should be noted, are those attributed by his onetime colleagues to Forbes himself upon his death.

"My recollection of what took place between us in 1843," Forbes continued in his private obituary

Forbes wrote four wills for Sophia Smith and served as her executor. It was in her final testament of March 8, 1870, that Smith provided for the women's college that still bears her name.

of Huntington, sympathetic it must be noted to the man's suffering and death due to consumption (tuberculosis), "made it impossible to me to do. And tho' in company (sic) with him between four and five years, the pleasure of the connection was constantly diminished by the necessity which was felt, and painfully too, of being constantly on my guard."

Attorney David Aiken then joined Forbes as a partner; this connection ended with Aiken's appointment in 1856 as a judge in the Court of Common Pleas. Forbes' third and last partner was Samuel Spaulding, and the firm of Forbes and Spaulding continued nine years until the latter was appointed Judge of Probate Court in Northampton. Actually, this partnership ended, according to Forbes' journal entry for July 5, 1864, before Spaulding's appointment to the Probate Court.

"Agreed with Spaulding," Forbes wrote, to dissolve the partnership existing between us. The position came from him ... that I should allow him a larger portion of the profits. I told him that my share was already so small that it was hardly worthwhile to diminish it and that It would be better to dissolve the firm. I wrote a notice of dissolution dated July 1, 1854, if I remember correctly." A few days later, Forbes writes: "Mr. Spaulding removed his books and furniture to the office he has taken ... .He took with him the receipts and letters of the firm and most of the stationery." Apparently no rancor existed between the two men, however, since Forbes would appoint Spaulding as one of the two executors of his will and one of the two trustees of his estate.

Although Charles Forbes himself no longer appeared in court during these years, he had many clients, nevertheless, who sought him out in connection with business matters and their wills. Thus, in collaboration with Deacon George Hubbard of Hatfield, a man skilled in business and financial matters but not an attorney, Forbes became involved in the founding of Smith College. At different times in her life, Forbes wrote four wills for Sophia Smith. It was in her final testament of March 8, 1870, that she provided for the women's college that bears her name. Forbes was not only appointed as an executor by Miss Smith; she also placed his name at the top of the list of men she wanted to serve as the first board of trustees of the college.

Forbes would, as a matter of fact,

attend the first meeting of the board of trustees of Smith College on April 12, 1871, at which — bringing his involvement to a close — he resigned. In his journal he would record the opening of the college four years later. The first entry, dated July 14, 1875: "Dedication and inauguration of Smith College." The second entry, dated September 9, 1875: "Opening of Smith College for Girls (sic). It is said that there were over two hundred applications for admission and only from fifteen to twenty admitted, the residue not being sufficiently advanced."

Three especially interesting recollections of his law practice, were recorded after Forbes' death, by young lawyers who knew or had come to know him — each in a different way. A newcomer to Northampton, D.W. Bond, discovered early on his arrival here that "the unbounded confidence that people seemed to have in his integrity and ability," was extraordinary. "It seemed to be taken for granted that any lawyer whose opinion did not correspond with that of Judge Forbes was not learned in the law." C. Parkman Judd admired Forbes because "he never encouraged petty law suits; he sought to avoid strife, and much as he loved the

Writing shortly after Forbes' death, Judge Daniel W. Bond noted "the unbounded confidence people seemed to have in his integrity and ability."

strife, and much as he loved the law, he always tried to check litigation. If his client was in the wrong, he told him so and urged upon him to agree with his adversary as soon as possible. He used to examine him through and through till the client would sometimes begin to think he was the culprit ... Hampshire County had very little litigation from 1830 to 1850, and this was largely due to the influence of Judge Forbes, Mr. Huntington and Mr. Baker." And almost like a benediction, Judd added, "Blessed was the client who followed the Judge's advice." During these years, Aiken believed, Forbes' income was never more than $2,000 a year which stressed the sagacity and prudence that guided his investments resulting in the estate that founded Forbes Library.

Another impression of Forbes was left by Col. William S.B. Hopkins, a Civil War veteran who had served with the 31st Massachusetts Volunteers. Hopkins was, incidentally, the son of preacher-politican Erastus Hopkins whom, as we shall see presently Forbes had so excoriated in his journal in 1849 during the Free Soil controversy. Forbes had despised the father, apparently, but liked the son who, as a young man, was welcome in his office. "When I was a young law student in Northampton," Hopkins wrote, "it was sometimes my habit to run in and see friends in the office of Forbes and Huntington or Forbes and Spaulding. In the morning, after papers had been read, the topics of the day discussed, I remember how Judge Forbes used to come in from his room. He never sat down, but putting his hands

behind him talked over the questions of the day, made suggestions as to this or that public man, and made such wise predictions in regard to all sorts of matters ... whether political, historical, or speculative subjects to which he had directed his attention, he seemed to be at home. He was a profound scholar ... Judge Forbes was a landmark in this community."

Chapter Four

"No Ordinary Man"

Fortunately, at the time of his passing in 1881, those who had known Charles Forbes sought also to record recollections of his appearance, private life, and character. These, together with his own faithful journal entries, bring us still closer to the man behind the Judge Forbes persona.

"In personal appearance," wrote Henry Burt who, in his youth as a *Gazette* apprentice had known Forbes in his prime, "he was a striking figure. Tall and erect, fully six feet in height and well proportioned with strong expressive features and a clear-cut face. He impressed one as being no ordinary man. He might not always have been ready with a pleasant word, or with levity of speech, but there was nothing forbidding in his appearance. He was one who seemed busy with his own thoughts as he went about the streets of the town. In the winter months, as he went forth on his daily walks, wrapped in his long cloak, he left the impression of one having unusual strength and grandeur of character. I still have a more vivid recollection of him than of any other of Northampton's public men."

As to how Forbes clothed his impressive person, there are in his papers a number of receipts from tailors and drapers, or clothing dealers, — also laundresses — indicating that Charles Forbes not only dressed in the best black cassimere (cashmere) and white linen but was also fastidious in his hygiene.

Not all 19th-century homes had indoor plumbing. Many people in Northampton relied instead on public facilities like the "Bath Room" advertised here, including, perhaps, Judge Forbes himself.

"His charming voice, exquisitely rich and musical, charming even the dullest listener,"{ was according to Charles Delano, "especially noticeable as no small element of his power and success ... and his smile was as winsome as a woman's." Timothy Spaulding, lawyer son of Forbes' partner for nine years, had been "accustomed from childhood to his manner and ways. His conversation was rich, forceful and elegant, and his manner fascinating. His charming voice, too, was one of the most clear and musical I have ever heard."

"He was a man who could unbend and often did," said Delano of Forbes. "He could talk on a level with the most learned" and then "descend to the chatter of the light-headed with the most delightful ease. He had a lively sense of humor, ready wit, and a pungent sense of sarcasm." For twenty years before Forbes' retirement, Delano had enjoyed the company of Charles Forbes, "join-

ing him in his daily morning and evening walks till thus together we traveled thousands of miles, revisiting again and again every highway and byway in Northampton. These walks and talks were in every vein of wisdom, wit, dry railery and playful humor." Delano had known Forbes "in his prime," he added, not just "on the strictly professional side ... but outside the court house ... with his rod and gun, his fishing tackle and game bag, exploring the fish ponds, threading the trout brooks ... traversing the forest and fields round about his favorite Northampton ... wherever there was prospect of game."

During the early and middle years of his life here in Northampton, Forbes' journal reflects the outgoing, sociable man that Delano describes. Although he later lost interest, Forbes joined the local Jerusalem Lodge of Masons and between 1819 and 1822 served three one-year terms

Judge Forbes enjoyed daily walks in the countryside around Northampton. As a onetime trustee of the city's Lunatic Hospital, he would have been familiar with this particular view of the city, painted in 1865.

44

In his diary, Forbes described a Fourth of July celebration on Round Hill in 1839, which included a "tea party and ball ... and rockets in the evening."

as Master of this lodge and as District Deputy Grand Master in 1827 and 1828.

Forbes' social life in this period was wide and varied. He describes a Fourth of July celebration in 1839: "Very pleasant day. Tea party and ball on Round Hill... .One thousand persons there. Balloon sent up by Mr. Jacquet. Rockets in evening. Very good music by Monson band." That same year he attended a series of lectures on Phrenology by a Mr. Burke — "an Irishman but lectures well."

Forbes belonged to a Glee Club, played the flute with the Unitarian Society choir and enjoyed baseball games such as one between "The Westfield and Northampton boys near the Great Elm in the lower meadows." In 1848 he made sev-

eral trips to Holyoke to view the new dam that powered burgeoning industries. At the time of his death in 1881 he would have, in his estate, stock issued by the

The Hon. Isaac Bates, U. S. Senator and good friend of Forbes, who enjoyed going on turkey shoots with him.

On March 13, 1850, Forbes attended the dedication of Northampton's new Gothic-Norman-Tudor Town Hall, designed by William Fenno Pratt.

Holyoke Water Power Company. Of his survey of the dam at mid-century he wrote: "The scale on which operations are carried on there is gigantic." In the autumn during these years, Forbes enjoyed turkey shoots with his friend, U.S. Senator Isaac Chapman Bates.

During the 1840s, Forbes was active in the local Temperance movement, one of the many social reforms flourishing in this period before the Civil War. He made many addresses in towns around the valley and records one on a November night in Whately: "A very good meeting." Unfortunately, he was interrupted by a drunken stage driver, named Hawks, whom men from the audience "dipped twice in a trough of cold water near the church."

On March 13, 1850, Forbes attended the gala dedication of Northampton's new Gothic-

Jenny Lind, the "Swedish Nightingale," and her husband as they appeared on their honeymoon in Northampton in 1842.

Norman-Tudor Town Hall, a romantic design by young architect William Fenno Pratt who would, before the century ended, leave his signature on much of Main Street. "Six hundred persons said to be present," wrote Forbes in his journal "Flagg's band of music from Boston and the celebrated bugle-player, Kendall." Forbes would also attend Jenny Lind's legendary concert there two years hence but without any comment as to her talent.

One local entertainment in this era did not sit well with Charles Forbes, a so-called "mock court," or trial, a popular nineteenth-century comic entertainment. Someone impersonating Forbes, sported a high collar extending up to his ears, an exaggerated copy of Forbes' own neckwear. This was a man he knew well, and it was said that he never spoke to that individual again. Forbes was not one to brook undue familiarity, and according to those who knew him well, such as David Aiken, was "a sensitive man." Timothy Spaulding considered Forbes "an unusually sensitive man" adding that "his power of analyzing men's motives from their acts was such that no imposture or charlatanry could stand before it. That phase of his character and temperament sometimes led him to abandon old friendship." That trait apparently grew more noticeable as Forbes aged. "He was best liked by those to whom he was best known," Spaulding maintained, "and to them his manner was kind and gracious."

On August 5, 1858, Forbes recorded the lively celebration here of the completion of the laying of the Atlantic Cable. "News

HAMPSHIRE GAZETTE.

NORTHAMPTON, AUGUST 10, 1858.

The Atlantic Telegraph Cable Laid!

Dispatches from Mr. Field to the President and the Press—The President's Reply—The Public Rejoicings—Our Own Congratulations.

The telegraphic wires conveyed with lightning speed to all parts of the country last Thursday afternoon, the gratifying intelligence that the Atlantic Telegraph Cable was successfully laid from the shores of Ireland to the shores of Newfoundland.

ANNOUNCEMENT TO THE PRESIDENT.

The President, who was at Bedford, Pa., received the first intimation of the successful laying of the Atlantic Cable through the agency of the Associated Press. The following is a copy of Mr. Field's Message to the President:—

TO THE PRESIDENT OF THE UNITED STATES.

*Dear Sir:—*the Atlantic Telegraph Cable on board the United States frigate Niagara and H. B. M. steamer Agamemnon was joined in mid-ocean July 29, and has been successfully laid, and as soon as the two ends are connected with the land lines, Queen Victoria will send a message to you, and the Cable will be kept free until after your reply has been transmitted.

With great respect, I remain,

Your obedient servant,

CYRUS W. FIELD.

On August 5, 1858, Forbes recorded the lively local celebration for the completion of the laying of the Atlantic Telegraph Cable, noting that "every church bell in town was rung for one hour."

of the laying of the Atlantic Cable," he wrote on August 5, 1858, "was received in Northampton on the fifth of August, 1858 in the afternoon. The Gazette had anticipated its arrival and made arrangements to issue an extra edition. As soon as the news arrived, a small sheet was issued announcing the great news. There was great excitement.... Everybody rejoiced. The great cannon was brought out and a salvo of thirteen guns fired.... Every church bell in town was rung for one hour."

Walking was, all of his life, one of Charles Forbes' greatest pleasures. Joseph Marsh, Forbes' bookseller on Main Street, recalled his patron's "stalwart form as he swung his cane on his daily walks through the streets of our city. I never saw him ride." On April 1, 1851, Forbes wrote in his journal. "Ground perfectly settled and has been for several weeks. Walking good in all directions." So regular were his twice-daily walks, it was said that people in houses along his customary routes could set their clocks by him.

One of Forbes' favorite routes was out Bridge Street to the Connecticut River and the bridge leading over to Hadley. On one of these walks he encountered a dog accustomed to successfully challenging all passers-by who sought to go by his house. Without word or gesture, Forbes turned, stalked

The Hockanum Ferry with Mt. Holyoke in the background. One of Forbes' favorite walking routes was out Bridge Street to the Connecticut River and the bridge leading over to Hadley.

back to his office on Main Street, picked up his pistol, walked back, put a bullet through the animal's head and went on his way. Ordinarily, his walks were apparently peaceful. Each spring he faithfully reported in his journal the appearance and condition of the Connecticut River with respect to the breaking up of the ice followed by the resulting freshets. "Went up to the Northampton bridge," he wrote on January 28, 1830. "Many of the boards are stripped off. Water has fallen about a foot... . The Montague bridge is gone — just built. Sunderland bridge also injured. Part of the Hartford bridge is also gone." The following spring he wrote late in March: "Went to Bridge. Ice cleared out above the bridge last evening but has not gone out at the Hockanum ferry. Blackbirds in flocks in the meadows. Robbins (sic) appeared some days ago."

Active in local politics, Forbes was, according to the *Gazette*, "a born Federalist, continued a Whig, was afterwards a Republican, and was always opposed to the Democratic party. He was not what we have come to understand by the term politician, though he was always ready to talk on political questions and used to go about talking on Sunday nights as was the practice when he was in his prime."

As a prominent Whig speaker, Forbes was asked in 1840, when Erastus Hopkins — a prominent Northampton preacher-politician — came out as a "Free Soiler", to refute him on election eve. In his journal, Forbes wrote, with his usual understatement: "Had occasion to speak of Erastus Hopkins, one of the candidates of the Free

Erastus Hopkins, 1840 candidate of the Free Soil Party, was described by Forbes as "a vain, heartless demagogue."

Henry Shepherd recalled Forbes referring to Erastus Hopkins during a pre-election meeting as "that old peacock!"

Civil War veteran Col. William S. B. Hopkins - Erastus Hopkins' son - was fond of Forbes in spite of Forbes' feud with his father.

HAMPSHIRE GAZETTE

The Fight Commenced.

We have entered upon that most horrible of horrors—Civil War! The rebel confederacy, in the most wanton and entirely inexcusable manner, commenced an attack on Fort Sumter, on Friday last, and after thirty hours bombardment, captured the fort. So this outrage upon the general government there is but one response from every true patriot—we must fight! The gage of battle has been thrown down by the rebels and we cannot do otherwise than accept it. The stars and stripes must be sustained and they will be. The time for forbearance has passed and there is nothing but war left. The north and north-west are all ready and all the men and money needed by government will be at once forth coming.

The general government is alive to the crisis and strong and decided measures will be at once taken to vindicate its authority. The president has issued a proclamation calling for 75,000 volunteers and called Congress together in extra session for the 4th of July, and the president has intimated to the Viginians that he may attempt to retake and hold the federal property, Fort Sumter included, and will probably cut off the mails to the South.

The northern states are nobly responding to the call of government and all the men needed to hold Washington against any force that the rebels could bring, will be at once forth coming. Gov. Curtin assures the president that he can put 100,000 men in Washington in 48 hours. Men are rapidly enlisting, and all party feeling is merged in patriotism. The New York legislature, just before its adjournment, on Saturday, passed the act appropriating $500,000 for arming and equipping militia to aid the federal government. The famous seventh and sixty-ninth regiments of New York have offerd their services to government. Ohio is enrolling 25,000 men, Gov. Sprague of Rhode Island has offered the general government the service of the marine artillery of Providence, and a thousand

CIVIL WAR!

Fort Sumter Captured.

SPIRITED DEFENSE OF MAJ. ANDERSON.

Fleet off the Harbor, but unable to Assist.

The rebels commenced the war on Friday last, by an attack on Fort Sumter. At 4 o'clock A. M. the batteries on Sullivan's Island, Morris Island and other points were opened on fort Sumter, and a brisk cannonading kept up during the day. Maj. Anderson did not reply, except at long intervals, till between 7 and 8 o'clock, when he opened with two tier of guns on fort Moultrie and the floating Battery. The issue was submitted to Maj. Anderson of surrendering when his supplies were exhausted or having fire opened on him within a certain time. The telegraphic correspondence between the rebel commander at Charleston and the government at Montgomery will be found below.

The firing of the rebels continued all night, at intervals, but Maj. Anderson ceased firing at 6 o'clock P. M. and was engaged in repairing damages during the night. The firing from fort Sumter recommenced on Saturday morning at 7 o'clock, the fort seemed to be greatly disabled; the battery at Cumming's point doing great damage. At nine o'clock a dense smoke was perceived to burst out from Fort Sumter. The federal flag upon the fort was at half-mast, as a signal of distress. Shells from Moultrie and Morris Island were falling into Anderson's stronghold thick and fast, and could be seen in their course at Charleston. The breach made in the fort was on the side opposite Cumming's Point. Two port-holes were knocked into one, and the walls from the top was crumbling.

The flames spread within the fort, and were seen bursting out of the portholes. Maj. Anderson sent out a squad of men to pass water to extinguish the flames. During the fire, the batteries of Sumter replied only at long intervals, the men were mainly engaged in putting out the flames. About 1 1-2 o'clock on Saturday, Maj. Anderson hoisted a white flag, and shortly afterwards surrendered the fort. During

During a political address in 1860, Forbes predicted the onset, and outcome of the Civil War one year before it actually began.

Soil Party, with some severity." Forbes then proceeds to label him "a vain, heartless demagogue ... aiming solely at his own ends. I felt it to be my duty to expose him." (This was, of course, the father of the Colonel Hopkins who had so admired Forbes — as a young law student — and who came back to Northampton for his funeral.) One onlooker of Forbes' "severity" towards the "Free Soiler" candidate Hopkins on that election eve in 1840, was one Henry Shepherd who recalled: "The old meeting house was as still as death when Forbes came to the peroration and a closing invective against the opposition party." Forbes paused, according to Shepherd, and then "thundered in a hoarse bass voice: 'As to Erastus Hopkins! That old peacock! We'll w-r-i-n-g his neck! W-r-i-n-g his neck! and bury *him* fifteen feet deep before tomorrow night!'" Hopkins, Forbes wrote in his journal, had vowed that if the Whigs proscribed him, he would "bury the Whig party fifteen feet underground."

Perhaps the most interesting of these political speeches of Forbes to have been recorded, was recalled by Colonel Hopkins: "I remember his delivering a political address in the town hall, I think in 1860, in which he discussed the great question of the day in a judicial manner while other people were discussing it in a passionate and excited way. He said: "A great many people say there is no danger from the South but, fellow-citizens, I fear there *is* danger, and I ask you to look with me at the facts and see what the result will be." That audience settled down to look with him into the face of the war that burst upon

them the next year. Judge Forbes said: 'The Southern people are used to out-door pursuits, they handle firearms, they always ride in the saddle, they are in the habit of pursuing exercise to a great extent; while the people at the north are too busy in the pursuits of trade to take much exercise, and that he predicted as a natural consequence that, in the early engagements of the war, the south would be victorious; but the great strength and the great wealth and the great patriotism of the north would in the end overcome it all.

Colonel Luke Lyman, whom Forbes suspected of padding his enlistment totals during the Civil War years.

That prediction in that town hall," concluded Hopkins, one of the men who had had to fight the Civil War, "told the exact story of Bull Run, Big Bethel and Ball's Bluff — and also the story of Antietam, Gettysburg and Appomattox."

Considering Forbes' prescience as demonstrated above, it seems strange that he included almost nothing concerning the Civil War in his journal jottings. One item concerns the funeral of Lt. Frederick Wright whose body had been shipped home for burial following his death in battle in Virginia in July of 1864. A second entry involves, in February of that same year, his donation of a $100 check to Colonel Luke Lyman "towards bounties for soldiers raised the present season." Forbes, after conversing with Lyman concluded that the latter had been padding his enlistment totals by including non-residents of Northampton plus some transients. "So much for the statements of Luke Lyman," Forbes wrote. On April 14, 1865, he noted "the assassination of President Lincoln at the theatre," and, unaware that secretary of state William Seward would survive his wounds, added, "and of Sec'y Seward at his house. The murderer of the Pres. is said to be known. His name is Booth."

Although Judge Forbes never appeared to be, or was considered a man of wealth, he was a canny investor and thus built up the considerable estate that surprised local citizens at the time of his death. From his annual income, that his friend Aiken believed never amounted to more than $2,000 a year, he made a steady series of investments. All through his journal are entries recording purchases of stocks and bonds. In 1839, he recorded the arrival in Northampton of the first canal boat of the New Haven and Northampton Canal Company. Five years later, in 1844, he would record selling five shares of stock in that company for five dollars apiece more than he had paid for them in 1836. That same day he attended a "meeting of the stockholders of the Northampton and Springfield railroad for the purpose of organizing the corporation. Stock all taken up. It is supposed the road will be made in a year." From this point on, there are frequent references to railroad stocks, the wave of the future.

A slow, methodical worker,

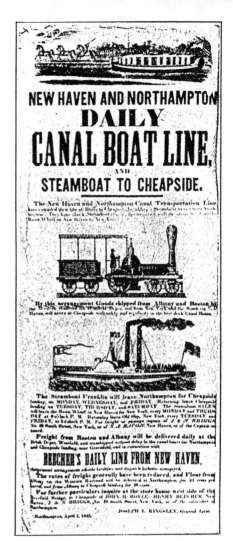

Forbes watched the first canal boat arrive in Northampton in 1839. He owned shares in the New Haven and Northampton Canal Company but sold them in 1844 at a handsome profit when he perceived that railroads were beginning to take over.

Forbes' success and profits came to him the hard way. "Why, there's Isaac Chapman Bates," he once remarked. "He will work all the week before court on his farm, and then come into court on Monday morning and make a better plea than I can after digging away for three months."

Although prudent and thrifty, Forbes lived well and was generous to his friends and even acquaintances. For example, young Charles Forbes Warner, named after the Judge, visited the latter before leaving Northampton, at age fourteen, to learn a trade at Cambridge. Before leaving town, he paid what he considered a courtesy call on his namesake. "My call was brief, and I merely stated to the Judge that I had called as a matter of duty and hoped his good health would continue. He thanked me and said he hoped that I would learn my trade well... . He then asked me to go upstairs with him, and in his room he took out his safe and presented me with a $250 watch, a Waltham, Appleton and Tracy movement, and he said, 'It is a good watch, keep your time by it. Be punctual and keep your appointments, and you will lay some of the foundations for success."

At the age of eighty and unwell, Forbes was the recipient of a wedding invitation from a daughter of his onetime partner, Spaulding. Unable or not wanting to attend, Forbes sent his regrets, concluding, "My presence at your wedding would be like a frost in July." But he enclosed a generous check for fifty dollars that presumably assuaged the bride's disappointment.

As he aged, traditional religion offered no comfort to Judge Forbes. Although he had been instrumental in founding the Unitarian Society in 1825, he ceased attendance in later years. There are repeated references to that church in the earlier decades of his life, however. "May 12, 1839, Mr. Barrett at the Unitarian Church Sunday. A young man and a long sermon." In July of that year he heard a Mr. Dwight: "Fine talents — appears most amicable. Has preached — this is the third Sabbath. Objections to him on account of his transcendentalism." Oddly, Forbes never mentions Ralph Waldo Emerson who is said to have preached several times at the church. Forbes was generous and faithful in his donations. He records his mounting annual contributions over the years that finally reached fifty dollars. On January 4, 1860, however, he writes: "Paid George Wright $50 for Society and said to him that

The Joseph Marsh bookstore stood near the corner of Main and Pleasant Streets. Joseph Marsh knew Forbes well as he spent a great deal of time in the shop.

the Society must not rely on me for the future." His pew, worth fifty dollars, he left to the Society in his will but no other bequest. "Of late years," reported the *Journal* at the time of his death, "he has not attended church much, though still clinging to a liberal view of religious matters."

It was Joseph Marsh, Forbes'

Main Street book seller, who believed he understood his patron's views of religion. Forbes was in and out of Marsh's shop from the time it opened in 1856 until his own death. "He had little faith in theology," said Marsh, "and was quick to discern the limitation of reason and the speculative nature of whatever went beyond the limits of reason. He told me on one occasion that he had helped build several churches but would give no more for that purpose, that he took no interest in proselytizing, that man's logical creed had very little effect upon his character, and that character was the supreme object of his life. He looked upon the Bible," Marsh added, "as a record of the thoughts of the time to which it was related and considered that the ancients had no binding authority upon the religious conceptions of the present day."

Marsh's description of Forbes' views on religion is substantiated by what remains today of the judge's onetime personal library — apart from his law library — originally containing some 3,000 volumes that formed the nucleus of Forbes Library.

What remains today, at the Forbes Library, of Judge Forbes' own library is a collection of more than 300 volumes. Most have been rebound, having been victims of the serious fire that hit the Forbes on March 26, 1942. All the others, presumably, were consumed through attrition over the years.

One can only speculate that many of Forbes' books were bought by him right here in Northampton. "I remember him very well as a book-buyer," said Joseph Marsh, "seldom buying anything but standard scientific works. On one occasion he told me to stop his Harper's Magazine as it was but trash. Occasionally, he expressed disappointment in a book which fell short of his expectations. His commanding intellect and judicial training made it easy to detect the superficial, illogical or absurd."

A survey of the titles of the remaining ten percent of Forbes' onetime personal library, verifies Marsh's belief in Forbes' "commanding intellect." The *Gazette*, too, extolled Forbes' intellectual curiosity and noted his endless reading. "He was an indefatigable reader up to the very last. He has lately watched and traced with great relish the development of advanced scientific theories. With the march of improvement he desired to keep abreast, and has been a great consumer of new books and magazines." In the Forbes' obituary the *Gazette* concluded with a reference to the old man's habit of reading late into the night: "His hours were late though regular, and the late passers on the street will miss the sight of his lighted rooms, in which he burned the midnight oil."

It is in the leftovers of Judge Forbes' own library that one probably comes closest to this remarkable man. The range and depth of his reading discloses that of his own intellect. Although his partner Aiken recalled that reading Harriet Beecher Stowe's *Uncle Tom's Cabin* "drew tears from his eyes," virtually all of Forbes' reading apparently consisted of non-fiction with a heavy emphasis on science. The titles fall under the modern classifications of anthropology, astronomy, botany, criminology, geology, health, mental disease (he was for a time a trustee of what was then called the Northampton Lunatic Hospital), meteorology, pathology, physiology and zoology. To the end of his life in 1881, Forbes was buying and reading the latest books in these fields as his copies, for example, of Charles Darwin's *Descent of Man* and Thomas Huxley's *Origin of the Species* revealed.

There are numerous books concerning language including Greek and Latin grammars and lexicons plus works in those tongues by Julius Caesar, Catullus, Cicero, Horace, Juvenal, Ovid and Aeschylus. These classics, he enjoyed in the original. "You can no more translate the orations of Demosthenes into English than you can translate Shakespeare into French or German," Forbes observed to a friend. He also read French.

Exploration, government, history and politics — both ancient and modern — are also heavily represented in Judge Forbes' library. He held John Stuart Mill, a number of whose works he owned, in high regard, and on the occasion of his death in 1873, labeled him "one of the best minds that England has ever produced."

Alongside books on the history of the Civil War, the French

Revolution and the Mexican War sits a copy of a book published in 1814: *Roman Antiquities* by A. Adam. And thereby hangs a tale. On December 29, 1843, Forbes described in his journal a visit from onetime *Gazette* editor Sylvester Judd, who as we know, had helped to deny him the Probate court judgeship he had sought nine years earlier. "P.M. Sylvester Judd in my office. Taking down and looking at books, reading some. So he went to the case at the left of the stove and took down several books. Then he went to the window to read one. After he was gone, I saw a space vacant on the shelf where stood, as I believe, Adams' *Roman Antiquities*. The book was gone." Shortly after, Forbes recorded finding the book on another shelf but added, "I am ignorant about what book did fill the vacant space." *Roman Antiquities* survived the 1942 fire at the Forbes Library — more of which later — and sits today, a bit water-stained and also rebound, among the remnants of the Judge's once vast collection of books.

Deeply involved in the growing nineteenth-century conflict between religion and science, Forbes

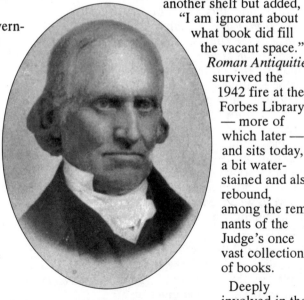

Sylvester Judd, onetime editor of the Hampshire Gazette. During a meeting in Forbes' office, Judd took down and looked at a number of books. After he left, Forbes thought he had gone off with one book, but later found it on another shelf.

The Reverend Nicholas Murray, who wrote under the pen-name "Kirwan," was the author of a virulent anti-Catholic treatise. Forbes had a copy in his collection.

owned a number of books on this subject as well as some on superstition and cults. Most notable among these is one published in 1852 by an Irish-born-Presbyterian convert from Roman Catholicism, the Reverend Nicholas Murray who wrote under the pen-name "Kirwan." Employing a common literary device of his time, Murray wrote a long and virulent anti-Catholic diatribe under this guise: *Letters to the Hon. Roger B. Taney, Chief Justice of the United States, or Romanism at Home.* To a nation still primarily Protestant in tradition and culture at mid-century, and whose children grew up reading *Fox's Book of Martyrs,* the hordes of immigrants now pouring into the country — many of them Irish Catholics — frightened them. Murray's book both fed and fueled this anti-Catholicism. Justice Taney, to whom Murray directed his argument, was a Roman Catholic.

"When Sir," thundered Murray, "the religion of the Bible is supplanted by the religion of legends ... by that religion that gives up all thinking to the priest — where the twenty-two or three millions of people .. in our happy land is supplanted by a people who believe all the lying legends of Romanism — then the last rays of our liberty are fading away on the summit of

our mountains. The midnight of liberty is the high noon of Romanism; and the deepest darkness of despotism is the paradise of the priest." Indeed, something of this is echoed certainly in that section of the will where Forbes referred to "the inroads of a foreign superstition, whose swarms of priests, Jesuits, monks, ministers, and agents" that he obviously believed were a threat to the public. As a younger man he had, too, been passionately moved by historian William Prescott's *Ferdinand and Isabella (1835)* in which he learned of the Inquisition under

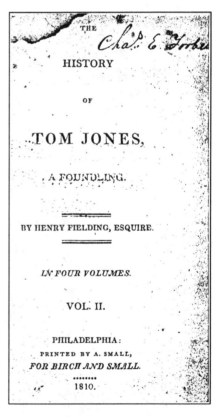

THE

Chas. E. Forbes

HISTORY

OF

TOM JONES,

A FOUNDLING.

BY HENRY FIELDING, ESQUIRE.

IN FOUR VOLUMES.

VOL. II.

PHILADELPHIA:

PRINTED BY A. SMALL,
FOR BIRCH AND SMALL.

1810.

Tom Jones, a bawdy 18th-century novel, was the only fiction book, that we know of, in Forbes' private library. His copy, with his signature inside, survived a fire at Forbes Library in 1942 and was later rebound.

Torquemada and the expulsion of the Jews from Spain. 'January 31, 1839. Read *Ferdinand and Isabella.* Expulsion of the Jews. vol 2, p. 135 et. Seq. Execrable. Most execrable! The Inquisition's Torquemada a fanatical scoundrel." Forbes, incidentally, despised Chief Justice Taney also excoriated by Murray. Upon Taney's death in 1864, Forbes wrote: "Died at Washington ... Roger B. Taney, Chief Justice of the Supreme Court of U.S. His great achievement was the decision of the Dred Scott case, every page of which shows him to have been a tool of the Slave Power, a contemptible, shuffling (devious) judge, a jesuit in politics as in religion."

How wonderful, then, in this sampling of what constituted Judge Forbes' library — most of it so relentlessly intellectual — to come upon this little volume: the rollicking bawdy eighteenth-century novel, written by Henry Fielding, himself a judge, *The History of Tom Jones, a Foundling.*

The other great passion of Judge Forbes' life, besides his books, was his collection of fine and costly timepieces. "Some men have wives and children," he once confided to a friend, "I have clocks and watches." There are repeated references in the journal to his new acquisitions. "March 6, 1841. Exchanged my large gold watch and key with B.E. Cook for a more modern and convenient French watch with the following engraved on the outside of the inner case. 'Wm. Burnett, French Exchange, London. No. 7348. Improved Detached lever. Three Ruby Palets. Compensating curb.' And with the watch are two dials,

one gold, the other silver — two sets of hands, two crystals, 2 mainsprings, and a case of wood to place it in so as to expose the face only. Gave my old watch, key

Halfway up the stairs in Forbes Library stands Judge Forbes' "Howard Clock," a regulator clock that cost Forbes $450 in 1872 (equal to about $25,000 today). Forbes noted in his diary that he intended it "for the use of the library should that go into operation under my will."

57

and thirty dollars in exchange." The gift to young Warner, mentioned earlier, was recorded by Forbes himself. "December 9, 1869. "Delivered to Charles Forbes Warner the Waltham Watch No. 190,315, which I purchased in July, 1867, for $250, as a present. He was named after me and is going to leave this place."

In 1872, Judge Forbes made what has to have been one of the major purchases of his life and what he referred to as "The Howard Clock." A custom-made "regulator" clock, made by Howard and Company of Boston, it cost $450 a sum that would be equal to about $25,000 today. For packing, the railroad freight bill, and "for bringing to office", Forbes paid out a carefully recorded $12.09. On December 6, 1872, he wrote: "Clock set running in the afternoon. This clock I intend for the use of the Library should that go into operation under my will." This, incidentally, is the first — and only — reference in his journal to the future Forbes Library.

For nine years — until the day of his death — "The Howard Clock" ticked away the waning days of Judge Forbes' time on this earth. Surely there is symbolic meaning in the fact that his last journal entry concerns this clock. "October 20, 1880. Regulator cleaned by Hathaway. He refused any compensation for the service." Three months and a few days later, Judge Forbes died. "The Howard Clock" sits today on a staircase landing in the Forbes Library.

Typical of the late Victorian era was this ad for J.A. Dower & Co., undertakers, of Northampton. Note the plumes on the hearse.

Chapter Five

"The Means of Learning, if They are Disposed to Learn."

After the death of Judge Forbes in 1881, thirteen years were to elapse before the library bearing his name would become a reality. During that time his bequest was allowed, as he had proposed, to accumulate for a decade. By the time the trustees began the building of the Forbes Library in 1891, the bequest totaled $491,446. While augmented that of Judge Forbes. Earle's gift of $50,000 was left to the city of Northampton and was intended to supplement the Aid Fund. "The fund shall be designated the 'Pliny Earle Fund'," said the will, "and the income used in the aid of the city of Northampton in defraying the current expenses of the Forbes Library, i.e., payment of the employees within and

Pliny Earle, M.D., pioneer head of the Northampton Lunatic Hospital, left $50,000 to Forbes Library while the building was still under construction. His will directed that the income should be used to pay employees, lights, fuel, etc., but "not the salary of the Librarian."
On the right is the original building of the Northampton Lunatic Hospital, circa 1858. Forbes was a trustee.

the library was under construction, the bequest of Dr. Pliny Earle, for twenty-one years the pioneer head of what was originally called the Northampton Lunatic Hospital, without, fuel, light, etc., but not the salary of the Librarian."

So impressed was the *Gazette* by this additional piece of philanthropy, one of its writers would

**Christopher Clarke, nephew of
the man who was the main
benefactor of Northampton's
first public library. Because of
Christopher Clark's opposition
to the plan, the Clarke Library,
as it became known after the
Forbes opened, did not merge
with the latter until 1915, after
his death.**

actually refer to it as the Forbes-
Earle library at the time of its dedication in 1894. Meanwhile, the
citizens of Northampton and the
students of Smith College continued their joint use of the
Northampton Public Library, or
Clarke Library. It was during this
same decade, 1881-1891, that two

major problems confronting the
future Forbes Library came out
into the open.

The first problem, involving the
inevitable predicament of two
public libraries in a single town,
enlisted the passion and energy of
Christopher Clarke, one of
Northampton's foremost citizens
during the second half of the nineteenth century. The second problem, with President L. Clark
Seelye as proponent, stemmed
from the intention of the trustees
of Smith College to now utilize
the facilities of the future Forbes
Library of Northampton as they
had, since the founding of the college in 1875, used the Clarke
Library — thus holding off the
building of a college library. All
told, save for a room set aside for
books in College Hall and later
one in Seelye Hall, Smith College
would utilize the public libraries
of Northampton for the college's
first thirty-five years of existence.

The two problems outlined above
soon fused to form one mutual and
vital concern which had to do with
the selection of the site for
Northampton's projected Forbes
Library. Understandably, the
Clarke Library faction wanted the
new library connected, or at least
adjacent, to their library in
Memorial Hall down on Main
Street. The Smith College faction,
on the other hand, naturally wanted the site of the new library to be
convenient to their campus. For
the latter's purposes an ideal site
was the so-called "Turner Lot" on
West Street, across from College
Hall, where the Forbes Library
was indeed eventually built.

The struggle of Christopher
Clarke, and his associates, to
assure the continuance of the

Apart from some small reference collections, Smith College did not have its own library until 1909. Instead, for 34 years, its students used the Clarke and Forbes Libraries.

Clarke Library would occupy him until his death in 1915. Only a fortnight after Clarke's death it was Charles Forbes Warner, the long-ago recipient of the gold watch from Judge Forbes, his namesake, who would propose combining the two libraries including the John Clarke Library fund. This was done. Christopher Clarke's passion was particularly personal for it was, as we know, the will of his philanthropist uncle, John Clarke, who had made the library possible; and it was his nephew who had been largely responsible for the construction of Memorial Hall to house it. Interestingly, Christopher Clarke would seek — and win — office as a trustee of the Forbes Library in which capacity he served from 1886-1889.

The institution of a free public library in Northampton began here, as it had in many New England towns early in the nineteenth century, with a small group of readers who formed what was often called a "social library." By 1846, this local group had evolved as the Young Men's Institute that operated a small library in the Town Hall. The first sizeable donor to this project was the legendary singer Jenny Lind who was persuaded to appear in rural Northampton, as well as in Springfield, through the efforts of young Christopher Clarke. At the close of her second successful concert in 1852 at the new Town Hall, designed by William Fenno Pratt, Lind wrote a $700 check to the Young Men's Institute for the purchase of additional books for their library.

In 1860, the Institute turned over its library, now operating in the new Town Hall, to the town of

Singer Jenny Lind at the time of her performances in Northampton. Forbes' only journal reference to her was that she was "all the rage." Lind donated money to the Northampton Public Library.

Northampton. The town then appropriated $25,000 toward construction of a free public library building provided that an additional $25,000 could be raised through public subscription. The Civil War (1861-65) intervened, but in 1867 John Clarke died leaving $40,000 "to the town of Northampton for the benefit of the Public Library in said town, for the erection of a suitable building, and the increase and maintenance of the Library and for no other purpose."

It was Clarke's nephew, Christopher, who raised the required $25,000 through nineteen large subscriptions ranging from $200 to $5,000 with the balance received from less wealthy donors. When the resultant $50,000 still was insufficient to construct the library, young Clarke went out and raised $4,000 more. Following this, the town voted an additional $16,000. Memorial Hall, built to house the Northampton Free Public Library, and in so doing to honor the town's eighty-eight Civil War dead, was dedicated in 1874. Near the end of his long life, Christopher Clarke would refer to "the Northampton free public library and Memorial Hall" as "the principal event in my life of public work."

During the thirty-four years between the publication of Judge Forbes' will and his own death, Clarke worked to keep "his" library intact and functioning. To mold public opinion, he relied on speeches, letters, interviews, articles, editorials and the sheer force

Judge Forbes recorded the Northampton Public Library's hours of operation in his copy of its 1874 catalogue. His registered-reader number was 517.

of his own charismatic personality. With reference to the controversy involving the site of the new Forbes Library, Clarke opined in 1887: "It would be a breach of faith if it should go on the hill. The Forbes Library may go there for all I care, but I think the Clarke Library will stay downtown."

Only eight months before the Forbes Library opened in 1894, Clarke published a long, impassioned appeal in the *Gazette* in which he quoted from his uncle's will and also from the deed to the land on which Memorial Hall had been built. "The city has no moral right," Clarke insisted, "to take this building for any other purpose than that for which the literal-minded men contributed their money." Moreover, he himself considered the Clarke Library site to be better suited than the Forbes to serve "the convenience and the comfort of the common people ... that they now enjoy in the Memorial Hall and Public Library building." Clarke and his supporters, called "the separationists," believed that the Forbes Library, if built on the Turner Lot, would become "an annex to Smith College."

Some sense of Memorial Hall's attractive features, hard to perceive now in its present state of deterioration and decay, are preserved in a description found in an 1870s Northampton directory:

"The most imposing portion of the building, the Memorial Hall itself, constitutes the main entrance. ... The floor is of marble, and the ceiling twenty feet high. It is cased in black walnut and ash, elaborately carved and highly finished. ... In the recesses are tablets containing the memorial records of our fallen soldiers." The Clarke Library occupied the large, raised main section of the building, and the reading room was down below on the ground level.

In its prime, the Clarke Library owned more than 40,000 volumes and loaned out more than 40,000 items each year. When the library was closed upon Clarke's death in 1915, all of the fixtures — including the books, loan desk and heavy oak bookshelves — were moved to the Forbes. The latter two items are seen today upstairs in the Art and Music Department, and occasionally — in a very old book — patrons come upon a worn and faded Northampton Public Library bookplate.

Judge Forbes was himself a steady patron at the Clarke Library. Preserved among the still extant remnant of his personal library one finds his bound, book-

The Turner House, which was demolished to make room for the Forbes Library.

type catalog of the Clarke Library with his signature and also the library hours inscribed inside the front cover.

At the time Judge Forbes' will was published in 1881, the *Journal* reported to its readers that: "The reason for this somewhat unexpected bequest, and the testator's complete ignoring of the present library is found in the fact that Mr. Forbes sometime since had a disagreement with the library authorities upon some matter, and he has not lately taken any books from there." It is said that at some point Forbes had pledged $1,000 toward the construction of the Memorial Hall library building and then later revoked this for reasons unknown.

Whatever the circumstances involved in Charles Forbes' turning his back on the Clarke Library, it is intriguing that the one and only mention in his journal, of that library, involves his gift, in 1860, of ten volumes of the *American Quarterly Review.* His disengagement from the Clarke Library apparently did not, however, diminish his personal regard for

the Reverend William Leavitt, pastor of the First Church who, for the first decade of its existence, served as chairman of the Library Committee and even devised a catalog system for the Clarke Library. This is especially interesting, of course, because of Forbes' contempt for clergymen in general. Found in his papers after his death was the following unexecuted memorandum obviously intended to be added to his will in that section where he had excluded any and all clergy from anything to do with his projected library. "And whereas in said last will and testament it is provided that none but laymen, etc., ... I hereby will and direct that the Reverend W.S. Leavitt, the minister of the First Church Society, in Northampton, be an exception to said rule, having full confidence in his impartiality, united to great literary and scientific acquirements and unusual executive ability." It must then have been mutual regard, and not merely a sense of duty, that had inspired Leavitt to deliver his moving eulogy at the funeral of the anti-clerical Charles Forbes.

As the Clarke faction continued its advocacy of the library on Main Street, proponents for the site of the future Forbes Library up on West Street, close to the college, began pushing hard. In 1885, President Seelye "went public," as it were, and published a letter in the *Northampton Daily Herald*.

"And now, it can no longer be a breach of confidence, if I state what my relations to the Forbes Library have actually been. Shortly after my coming to Northampton, it was intimated to me by the late Judge Spaulding that, before using the limited funds of the college for a library, it would be well to ask the advice of Judge Forbes. I accordingly called upon him, fearing lest my visit might be resented as an intrusion; but was courteously received, and advised not to

faithfully than those who were dependent on the caprices of popular elections; but he said he had fully made up his mind that his library should be a separate institution, assuring me, however, the interests of Smith College should be well cared for, as he had already appointed two of its trustees — Deacon Hubbard and Judge Spaulding — as trustees also of his library. To them he should give the exclusive right to fix the location and to erect upon it a suitable building."

Seelye's suggestion to Judge Forbes that the trustees of Smith College would make better trustees of the library than "those dependent on the caprices of popular elections" had obviously fallen on deaf ears. Judge Forbes never removed or revised his anticlergy provision in the will, and it

A bird's eye view of the Forbes Library while under construction. As specified in Judge Forbes' will, the building was to be as fireproof as was humanly possible.

expend our funds for that purpose. Then, to my surprise and gratification, he confided to me the substance of those plans which his will has since made public. Their design coincided so fully with my own desires that I suggested the trustees of the college might execute it with less friction and more

must be remembered that L. Clark Seelye was himself an ordained Congregational minister.

As the library-site controversy continued, proponents of the Turner Lot, on which Smith College had an option, zeroed in on Forbes' provision in the will involving fire-proof considera-

The new library viewed from the College Hall tower. As a Hampshire Gazette writer observed at the time, : "the style of the architecture is modern. ... Above the large and imposing entrance is the inscription, Forbes Library." Many Northamptonians called it "the castle on the hill."

tions. He had insisted that "the building be fireproof ... and so disconnected from all other buildings as not to be endangered by fire originating in them." Memorial Hall, they pointed out, was "in no sense fire proof" with all its "floors, studding, laths, shelves, studs, roof-boards and other materials of wood."

An additional argument in favor of the Turner Lot involved cost. The ground next to Memorial Hall might come as high as $50,000, while the Turner Lot was being offered at $20,000. The choice of the latter was further expedited by an anonymous donor, who later proved to be Forbes trustee William Gaylord (appointed to replace George Hubbard who died in 1888), offering to contribute $5,000 toward the purchase of the lot. Smith College then relinquished its option, and the Turner Lot was purchased.

"After visiting many large libraries," in his own words,

Gaylord himself sketched a tentative floor plan for the Forbes Library and then hired Architect William Brocklesby of Hartford to design it. Other designs in Northampton, by this same architect included nine buildings for Smith College and also the Academy of Music.

"Judge Forbes wanted a fireproof building," the *Gazette* would report at the time of its dedication, "and he has it. No one doubts the indestructibility of the building. It has wood floors on top of thick cement, and these might take fire, but if they should burn the floors would stand. Sometimes heat expands a building so that its iron beams pull off their supports, but this building does not depend on beams. Its floors are held up by five brick arches (Guastavino arches) on brick pillars. No heat expands them, and fire does not destroy. The side walls contain no wood, but plaster is put on fire clay tiling, made porous to act as a non-conductor. The roof, too, is indestructible. It is slate, tiling, iron and copper. The builders have done well, and their structure is the kind whose architecture will wear well."

Moving inside, the *Gazette* writer observed: "They have not sacrificed light and room and utility to adopt a prevailing fad in architecture. ... The stranger will hardly need to ask if the building is for a library; it looks like it. It is just the same on the inside; utility is stamped on everything. The high vaulted ceilings show the fluted sides of the cream-colored fire clay tile used in their support, and the very white mortar in which they are pointed gives a pleasing look. The long red tiled hall and the heavy oak carvings and stairs look solid and lasting. ... Milford granite and Longmeadow red sandstone trimmings give an excellent color to the exterior. The front of the library is broken by about 30 large windows while either side and rear have nearly as many, or 150 in all. The style of architecture is modern. ... Above the large and imposing entrance is the inscription, Forbes Library."

In appearance, the Forbes exemplifies the so-called "Richardsonian" style inspired by the work of Henry Hobson Richardson, one of this country's premier nineteenth-century architects, whose influence is seen also in our Hampshire County courthouse. "A castle on a hill" is how many Northamptonians see the Forbes Library on their early childhood visits, which is as good a description as any of the majestic presence of the Forbes on its spacious grounds. The building itself has, over the years, proved remarkably adaptable to changing times and needs.

So well pleased with the new Forbes Library over which he would preside for nine years was the first librarian, Charles Ammi Cutter, — more of whom later, — that he would write in his last annual report in 1902:

"The Forbes building has contributed to the success of that library. Well placed in the centre of ample grounds, substantially built in an agreeable semi-romanesque style, it is unlike other libraries in that its whole lower story, 100 feet square, is a single room broken only by the pillars and arches that sustain the second floor. Older libraries look confined, dingy, and gloomy compared with this new, bright, open, cheerful building, and many of later date are not as home-like and comfortable."

Upon the successful completion of the building in 1894, the trustees themselves hailed their own achievement in the *Gazette*. The library "is estimated to accommodate 400,000 volumes, is unusually well adapted for library purposes, and is an ornament to the city and praised by all visitors." Its final cost was $134,529.

On the evening of October 23, 1894, the formal dedication of the Forbes Library took place. The next day the entire front page of the *Gazette* was devoted to the event that was held upstairs on the as yet unoccupied second floor. "Forbes Library. It Is Now Ours To Fight Over And Pay For" proclaimed the headline. "Last night the library was formally turned over to the city in the presence of 500 people," the article reported. Seated on a raised platform were:

Trustees William Gaylord, Oscar Edwards and George Ray; civic leader Arthur Watson; President Seelye; Architect William Brocklesby; Amherst College Librarian D.W. Fletcher; Librarian Charles Cutter; library Secretary Samuel Lee; author George W. Cable; Mayor Henry Kimball; and library Treasurer Frederick Macomber.

Charles Ammi Cutter, first librarian at Forbes, 1894-1903. In 1876, he wrote *Cutter's Rules for a Dictionary Catalog*, which became the world's leading textbook on systematic dictionary cataloging and partial model for the Library of Congress system itself.

A host of local clergymen augmented the number above; The Reverend Henry Rose, First Church; The Reverend Paul Van Dyke, Edwards; The Reverend Asa Dilts, First Baptist; the Reverend Frank Pomeroy, Methodist; the Reverend Roland Smith, St. John's Episcopal; the Reverend Frederic Hinckley, Cosmian Hall; the Reverend Richard Griffin, Unitarian; Father Patrick Gallen, Annunciation; and Father Thomas Lucey, St. Mary's. "Our trustees started off pretty heavily with ministers of religion and even had prayer," observed the *Gazette*. "It may be well to give the ministers considerable latitude at the start, as the will

prohibits their having anything to do with it, (the library) hereafter."

One of this clerical brotherhood, as well as president of Smith College, Seelye now took full advantage of this latitude as the major speaker of the evening. His remarks, as a matter of fact, took up most of the *Gazette's* front page. He began by commending the library trustees on "their work" and then went on to congratulate Smith College "on having at last an opportunity for literary research such as few colleges in this country enjoy. Naturally its students and teachers have a great interest in this library." He does not mention the fact that sixteen years earlier, in 1878, the college's lack of adequate library facilities was already being acknowledged in the *Smith College Circular*. "We greatly need a library for reference use.

"Books are the students' food; scholarship cannot prosper without them," Seelye informed the Forbes Library's dedication audience. "In these days successful teaching depends more and more upon ready access to the best literature. One of the first and most difficult problems of my administration was to supply this need. Although the city, indeed, was furnished with an unusually good public library, it was inadequate to meet the demands of advanced scholarship. The college funds were too meager to properly supplement it." Between 1875 and 1894, the college had, however, managed to build College Hall and a house for the president, plus

The original boilers that heated the Forbes Library were made, as this photo reveals, by S.W. and A.R. Lee of Northampton (later the Norwood Engineering Co.). The awarding of the contract to this particular company might today be viewed as somewhat questionable since at the time, Samuel W. Lee was also the library Secretary (1894-1905).

three classroom buildings, an art gallery, a gymnasium and an observatory. More than one dozen student residential houses were also acquired or built.

"In my perplexity," continued Seelye, "I consulted Judge Spaulding, one of my trustees. He advised me to consult Judge Forbes, intimating that he had a plan, known only to two of his trusted friends, which might relieve me and modify somewhat my plans. I did so, and the judge stated to me, confidentially, his intentions. In language similar to that of his will, he said his design was to furnish the best opportunity for scholars in every department of learning to gain the knowledge they needed from an extensive collection of books. He advised me, therefore, not to use our funds for that purpose any more than was necessary to meet our immediate needs, saying that although the library he intended to found would probably be under the exclusive direction of the trustees appointed by the town, he saw no reason why it might not be equally serviceable to Smith College." Seelye does not refer to his attempt, in 1885, to persuade Forbes to have the trustees of Smith College also control the Forbes Library.

At this point in his remarks, Seelye referred to previously expressed concerns by "some persons" at the time the site was selected, that "an undue advantage had been taken of the city by the college, and that its interests had been cared for at the expense of the city's." Seelye absolved himself of any responsibility for the selection of the Turner Lot site. "I was as much surprised as the rest of the community." He was, moreover, confident that "the jealous feeling which the choice of location excited in some minds has already subsided, and I am confident in a few years will entirely disappear."

Continuing in this vein, Seelye asked, "Does its proximity to the college endanger its usefulness? ... He certainly intended his library should be of the greatest possible service to the college as well as the city. ... Smith College, like this library, is a public charity. ... It is organized and administered solely for the public good. If it prospers, the city prospers with it; should it suffer loss, the city would be proportionately impoverished."

Seelye then went on to remind Northamptonians of jobs provided during the construction of the college buildings, of the "many thousands of dollars expended for land and buildings." as well as the annual distribution of "more than half a million dollars in trade."

The city, he pointed out moreover, was actually the recipient of "benevolence" from "persons living outside of Northampton." It was not "for these things alone," he hastened to add, "that the college deserves your consideration." The college, he pointed out, "offers to rich and poor alike, without distinction of creed or condition, a higher education than the public schools can offer at about half its actual cost. For those who cannot afford to pay the half, it gives through its scholarships, tuition without charge. The daughters of poor mechanics and day-laborers are freely educated and treated with as much consideration as the daughters of the rich." Benefits to Northampton, he

The Forbes Library staff, 1898. Librarian Charles Cutter is third from the left in the middle row.

70

pointed out, also included such educational advantages as the college art gallery, its exhibits, its botanic gardens, its courses of lectures and musical recitals. "The entire social life of the community is elevated and quickened by its presence," declared Seelye, and "we shall all rejoice that through the generosity of Judge Forbes, with no loss to the city, this new library has been brought so near the college and can administer so abundantly to its need." A few words of praise for libraries in general — the so-called "people's university" — and President Seeley was finished.

Also on the program as speakers that evening were Melville Dewey, superintendent of the New York state library school at Albany, and father of the Dewey Decimal System, who spoke only briefly as did Charles Cutter, the new first librarian of the Forbes and himself a noted figure in American librarianship. Dewey's remarks took up a single short paragraph in the *Gazette*; Cutter's took two.

For some reason, the *Gazette* writer who covered this event perceived a problem in the controversial site. "There is one drawback," he wrote, "and that is the music rooms of the college from which are wafted the clattering sounds of a dozen pianos and the warbling and screeching of a dozen hearty maiden voices. These may be heard on a still autumn day on the opposite bank of the Mill River."

One of the great moments in librarianship in this country had already occurred on August 1, 1894, — as the Forbes Library was nearing completion — when the trustees offered the position of

librarian to Charles Cutter, and he accepted. Cutter was already a national figure before he came to Northampton. During his distinguished twenty-five years at the Boston Athenaeum he had devised many badly needed and still-functioning library devices. The most important of these was doubtless his system of classification, for as he himself wrote in a *North American Review* article in 1869: "A large library uncatalogued is like a large city without a directory." *Cutter's Rules For A Dictonary Catalog*, published in 1876, would become the world's leading textbook on systematic dictionary cataloging. Based on letters of the alphabet, rather than the decimal system invented by Dewey, Cutter's system allowed for more minuteness of classification and in time would become the partial model for the Library of Congress system itself. Also at the Boston Athenaeum, Cutter devised other familiar library practices including: loan cards placed in a pocket pasted inside the rear cover of books; training classes for library assistants; an inter-library loan program; home deliveries of books to persons "who cannot visit the library." During these busy years he was instrumental in founding the American Library Association in 1876 and served twice as its president. The *Library Journal* claimed him as editor from 1881-1893, and he turned out a steady stream of articles, papers and bulletins. All his life, he continued his labor on his gigantic classification scheme for the logical classification of all knowledge, — nine thick volumes of which — he would leave unfinished in the Librarian's office at the Forbes Library at his death.

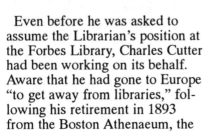

Even before he was asked to assume the Librarian's position at the Forbes Library, Charles Cutter had been working on its behalf. Aware that he had gone to Europe "to get away from libraries," following his retirement in 1893 from the Boston Athenaeum, the Forbes trustees had commissioned Cutter to purchase "foreign books and photographs" for the new library. For this purpose, they allotted him $50,000; a year later they would offer him the position as librarian.

In 1931, William Cutter, who

succeeded his uncle as librarian at the Forbes, would write of this happy marriage between his uncle and the new library in Northampton: "Here was an opportunity for which he had been waiting. All his pet schemes long held in abeyance could be tried. A book collection could be made *de novo*; he could finish the classification, apply the rules without criticism, and above all develop his ideas as to how a library should serve the public. In Europe he bought not only books but also pictures and music, for he determined to develop an art and music department side by side with the book collection. There have been few such opportunities. There was no book committee, no faculty, no school committee to interfere with him. The trustees had the then unusual idea that they had hired a librarian to make a library."

Cutter himself, in his first annual report, preserved a recollection of his first summer at the Forbes before the dedication in the autumn of 1894. "I began work, with a janitor and three assistants, in the Forbes Library, which was just out of the builder's hands, not even having a chair or table, nothing in fact within its walls but unpacked boxes of books, some 3,000 books which I had bought during the previous three months in Paris, Geneva, London & Boston." The trustees had granted him a far-reaching mandate to include: "The general charge, management, and control of the library and all persons therein. He shall have custody of all property, real and personal owned by and under control of the corporation for which no other provision shall be made." The trustees, under the Will, had turned over to the elect-

ed board of trustees the building that had cost $134,529, the Aid Fund of $20,000 with accumulated interest of $2,858, and the Book Fund that with an income accumulation of $40,042 now totaled $294,000.

This rare opportunity to actually create a library soon disclosed to Cutter the problems inherent in the small operating fund. He could, for example, hire only five assistants to help him to ready the library for the planned opening to the public on January 1, 1895, two months after its dedication. His original staff, besides the janitor, consisted of five young women — willing but as yet untrained in library work: two Smith College graduates; two high-school graduates; and a stenographer. They were paid $5.00 per week. Cutter soon established a weekly council where he and his staff together worked out their problems and created policy for the library. Realizing that the January 1 opening was not possible, the staff arranged an exhibit of books and art in November and announced the opening would take place July 1, instead.

As new books flooded in to join the already uncatalogued backlog of books, and with only one third of the library's holdings catalogued, Cutter arranged a makeshift system whereby the remaining two thirds were at least filed under two dozen classes and arranged alphabetically under authors' names. Cutter's requests for more funds and staff were not met, and by 1898 only 18% of the collection was properly catalogued. A concomitant problem, Cutter soon realized, was that: "Just as one of the staff is approaching higher efficiency, she may be carried off by a richer library or a husband."

Completed catalog or not, Cutter decided not to wait. "It was a bold experiment to commence to circulate books with practically no catalog," he would later report, "but it seemed better to give citizens the use of the library for which they had waited so long, even if they were put to some inconvenience, than to keep them out of it longer." Criticism by users was soon followed by sniping reported in the *Springfield Union*: "White elephant." ... Much Dissatisfaction With Forbes Management." The problem was solved, partly, in 1902, with the library's adoption of the Library of Congress card system.

Early patrons of the Forbes Library, despite the initial cataloging problem, were fortunate indeed. For one thing they were endowed with open stacks where they were free to wander, to browse, and to select books unhindered. "Our library is not a cemetery for dead books," said Mr. Cutter. The librarian, he believed, "is not a book watchman, nor a registry clerk, but a teacher of reading, an intellectual advisor, a mental doctor for the town. ... He is to be, in a literary way, the city physician and must be able to administer from the bibliothecal dispensary just that strengthening draft that will suit his case." Cutter, in short, believed that a library should be both a physical and spiritual oasis as well as "the center of culture in its town."

During his nine glorious years at the Forbes, Cutter practiced his belief that library policies should be based on what he termed the "watch-words" of "liberty, sim-plicity, elasticity and utility." Books were to be bought, and made easily and freely accessible to "our clients for amusement and knowledge and mental stimulus and spiritual inspiration" — not to satisfy merely the taste of the librarian, or a book committee, or as he put it, to "keep the shelves warm." A library, he maintained, "should be a practical thing to be used, not an ideal to be admired."

With Cutter's advanced and enlightened philosophy, plus Judge Forbes' generous and independent book-fund, patrons of the Forbes library were blessed indeed. They could, for example, request the purchase of books they wished to read; they could ask for books to be reserved for them. Instead of a single book at a time, Forbes patrons could withdraw several books — or combinations of books and magazines. As Northampton's foreign-born population grew, books in other languages were added: 2,500 volumes in French and 1,250 in German near the end of the century. By 1902, books in Yiddish, Polish, Italian and Spanish were being added.

At the Forbes Library, Cutter introduced an inter-library loan arrangement, a traveling library to reach small towns in Western Massachusetts, and established book-delivery stations in Florence, Leeds and Bay State. New books, roughly classified, were laid out on tables for patrons to choose from. In 1902, he set up a separate Art and Music Department with 50,000 items recorded in its own catalog. That same year he brought a children's room into being. At the time of Cutter's death in 1903, the Forbes Library boasted a registration of 5,784 or 31% of Northampton's population. A total of 108,871 books circulated that year from the library's collection of 96,974 volumes. Also loaned were 13,924 pamphlets; 4,214 pieces of sheet music; 54,086 photographs and engravings, and 1,055 newspapers.

At Charles Cutter's funeral in 1903, the Reverend Frederick H. Kent, Unitarian Society, observed that he would always be remembered as "a man going with a book in his hand to find a person whom the book could help."

Chapter Six

Five Librarians:
Their Trials & Triumphs
1904 - 1982

℘

In 1904, Charles Cutter's nephew, William Parker Cutter, Chief of the Order Division at the Library of Congress, was recruited to follow in his uncle's footsteps as Librarian of the Forbes Library. "The library and the city are fortunate in obtaining him," announced the trustees.

Awaiting Cutter on his arrival at the Forbes was a librarian's nightmare: a serious lack of shelving for the ever-growing book collection and a vast backlog of books not yet catalogued. Both problems stemmed from the inadequacy of the Aid Fund to support the library's operating expenses and the city's failure to live up to the terms of Judge Forbes' will with supplementary funds. In his annual report in 1901, Charles

In 1904, William Parker Cutter, nephew of Charles Cutter, succeeded his uncle as Forbes Librarian. Awaiting him on his arrival was a serious lack of shelving and a vast backlog of uncatalogued books.

Cutter himself had focused on "the small provision which the Forbes Library has for running expenses, with so large a book-buying income. In no library reports does one find less spent for management than for books; often the amount is half as much again and sometimes double." At the same time, he pointed out, "the circulation of the Northampton libraries is, in proportion to population, much larger than that of any other city in the United States, and the largest part of this circulation comes from the Forbes Library."

In his effort to solve the book-shelving crisis, William Cutter, during his tenure from 1904 to 1911, repeatedly sought a $25,000 appropriation from the city to provide a two-story steel stack system to replace the long-since outmoded one-story wooden stacks installed on the main floor when the library was built in 1894. Routinely, these requests were denied despite reminders that the city had agreed, on accepting Judge Forbes' gift, "to pay all expenses necessarily incurred in

Library in New York.

Stymied in his attempt to deal with the shelving problem, Cutter nevertheless applied himself to the great backlog of uncatalogued books that still plagued the library. His uncle's belief that adoption of the Library of Congress card system in 1902 would solve the problem at the Forbes had proved

Circa 1905: William Cutter's staff poses on the front steps of the library.

and about the management and administration of the affairs of said library" and even to "erect and provide such other building or buildings as may hereafter become necessary in consequence of the enlargement of the library." Cutter's pragmatic solution was to cut back by about two thirds on book purchases. "Unless we pile books on the floor, further purchases are impossible," he declared.

In 1916, the city would finally appropriate the sum needed for the steel-stack system still functioning at the Forbes today, but by this time William Cutter would have been gone five years. In 1911 he had resigned to become librarian of the Engineering Societies

overly optimistic. In 1903, the year of Charles Cutter's death, as a matter of fact, there were still 84,422 books uncatalogued out of a collection of 96,974.

By the time of his resignation in 1911, William Cutter could boast of what was probably his major contribution at the Forbes, — "that of our collection of 113,607 volumes, 98,407 are now completely catalogued."

Another recurring theme during William Cutter's tenure involved the steady loss of the Forbes Library's well-trained young female "assistants," as they were called, who were constantly being recruited for better-paying jobs in other libraries. "The training gained in this library has become so well known," reported Cutter, "that our assistants are in constant demand. Every assistant accepting a position elsewhere has bettered herself." At the Forbes Library, in 1910, the salaries of these women were in the two-to-four hundred dollar per annum range. Only a single assistant's salary of $626 came close to that of the janitor's $650. Just as his predecessor had done, Cutter pinpointed in all his annual reports the financial problem underlying all others at the Forbes. "The Aid Fund is not sufficient to pay the legitimate running expenses," he wrote in 1905.

Already looming at this time was another crisis: the problem of too few staff to deal with the burgeoning clientele of the Forbes that included, as we already know, not only the citizens of Northampton itself but also the faculty and students of Smith College. In addition to servicing these two major elements, the Forbes was also operating a medical library for local physicians, mounting frequent art and photo exhibits, and regularly delivering books to local schools, to Lilly Library in Florence, and to book "stations" in Bay State, Leeds, Pine Grove, Loudville, Smith's Ferry and West Farms.

Thus was William Cutter's watch enlivened by a stormy contretemps with Smith College in the person of President Lucius Clark Seelye. This confrontation that had been simmering for almost a decade finally boiled over in 1905. In his President's Report, Seelye was still assuring trustees of the college, now more than two decades old, that "the Forbes Library and the City (Clarke) Library, with their commodious rooms and magnificent funds, satisfy in large measure the demands for books and obviate the necessity of an extensive and very costly (college) library." That

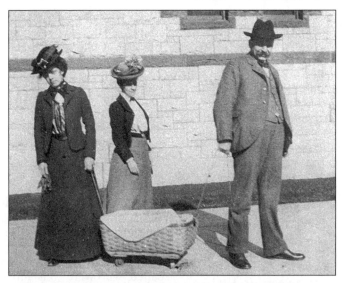

Three of the Forbes staff with wheeled basket, en route to one of the library's book "stations" in Bay State, Leeds, Pine Grove, Loudville, Smith's Ferry or West Farms.

In the January 1896 issue of the Smith College Monthly, student Elizabeth Warren, Class of 1899, commented: "Anyone whose sense of propriety or regard for the grass forbids her running down the bank below the side gate nearest College Hall in order to cross directly to the library, must take a wide detour ... why could there not be some steps down the bank at this convenient point?" The steps are still there today.

same year, however, Librarian Charles Cutter of the Forbes Library was reporting to his trustees the ever-increasing stress created by Smith students swarming across West Street to the Forbes to use the "reserve books" assigned in their classes. "They come for them in crowds," Cutter wrote. "They press forward ... expecting prior attention." The *Gazette* had earlier expressed fear that the college students " with their fine clothes and fine manners ... would keep the people of common clay away because they would not feel at home." It was not their fine clothes and manners that proved a problem, however, but rather the sheer weight of their numbers. The Springfield *Republican* estimated that two full-time "assistants" were needed solely to serve Smith students. After prodding by Librarian Cutter, the college did —between 1902 and 1905 — bestow an annual $500 gift on the Forbes. This, according to Seelye, was "gratefully received."

In 1905, confronted for the second successive year with a substantial deficit, the Forbes Library trustees now requested from Smith College an annual contribution of $2,500 to go toward the library's operating expenses. Immediately there started up a town-versus-gown battle, waged primarily in print, that lasted from April through August. Chosen to champion the Forbes Library's cause was Trustee Arthur Watson, a Northampton lawyer, and in him President Seelye finally met his match. In the ensuing barrage of communiques exchanged by Watson and Seelye — all of which were eventually published in the *Gazette*, Watson assailed all of Seelye's positions beginning with the latter's conviction that Judge Forbes had indeed intended the library to serve the college as well as the city. Seelye was certain, moreover, that if Forbes had foreseen this recent action of the trustees, he would have given the library to the college to begin with. Also, he deplored this "apparent antagonism to an institution which is doing as much as Smith College to increase the wealth and intelligence of the inhabitants of Northampton." The request of the library's trustees for

Forbes' trustee Arthur Watson, who endeavored to get Smith College to make a modest payment to the library, on which its students depended so heavily for three decades.

means something more than a person having a domicile. It implies citizenship and municipal relations ... and is subject to particular burdens." Watson next demonstrated that in no way had Forbes provided for any control of the library by Smith College had Northampton

an annual $2,500 contribution was met by Smith College with a counter offer of $2,000.

Watson now closed in. First, he challenged Seelye's premise that the students of Smith College were, as "inhabitants" of Northampton, beneficiaries of Judge Forbes' will just the same as the citizens of Northampton. Watson zeroed in on the will and the Judge's words "inhabitants of Northampton" to designate the recipients of his gift. In his own copy of the *Massachusetts Reports,* Forbes had, Watson discovered, underlined this definition. "The term inhabitant, as used in our laws and in this state,

Two young Forbes Library "assistants" circa early 1900s.

refused to accept his gift since, in that event, the money was to go to Harvard College — not Smith.

Watson kept up the attack. He determined that Amherst College, one half the size of Smith, was having to pay out $9,700 a year to operate their college library. Watson also learned, from the U.S. Commissioner of Education, that for the previous five years Smith College had managed to save, from income, $80,000 a year. The Forbes trustees now rejected Seelye's offer of an annual $2,000 and instead voted that each Smith student, not an inhabitant of Northampton, be required to pay an annual $5.00 fee — in advance — to use the library.

In late October, the controversy between the Forbes Library and Smith College subsided somewhat when a mysterious anonymous donor offered to add the extra $500 to the college's $2,000 contribution. This would be carried out for three years at the end of which the annual $5.00 student fee would begin. A new era, however, was dawning. Finally, after thirty-five years of dependence on the city of Northampton's two public libraries — especially the Forbes

Joseph LeRoy Harrison, third Librarian at the Forbes. A one-time newspaper man, he stayed for thirty-eight years, through two world wars, the golden twenties and the great depression of the 1930s.

— Smith College decided to build itself a college library which would open in 1909.

Successor to William Cutter at the Forbes, in 1912, was Joseph LeRoy Harrison, a onetime newspaperman and a graduate of the library school founded at Columbia University by Melville Dewey. Librarian for seventeen years at the Providence Athenaeum, Harrison was recruited by Cutter as Librarian for the Forbes where he would serve for thirty-eight years including two world wars, the golden twenties and the great depression of the1930s.

Harrison was to leave his mark on the Forbes in many ways beginning with the hiring of the first children's librarian. Through this means he sought also to reach the large immigrant population of Northampton. Besides serving the children, this department purchased books in Polish and

Yiddish, for example, for youngsters to take home to their parents. Regular visits were made to schools to encourage children to come to their room on the library's second floor.

In 1916, there finally took place the inevitable amalgamation of Northampton's two public libraries. For twenty-one years after the founding of the Forbes Library in 1894, primarily through the force of his personality and popularity, Christopher Clarke had kept alive the Northampton Public Library, commonly known as the Clarke Library after his uncle whose bequest had been instrumental in founding it. In 1915, Christopher Clarke died, aged 88, and in less than a fortnight the proposal was made to at last merge the two libraries. Interestingly, the proposal came from editor-publisher Charles Forbes Warner whom we met in an earlier chapter as a budding printer's apprentice receiving his going-away gift of a gold watch from Judge Forbes. Warner had returned to his native Northampton where he found work as a journalist and then for sixteen years served as editor of the *Hampshire County Journal.* On April 6, 1916, the Northampton City Council voted to phase out the Clarke Library and directed that all books, equipment and income from the John Clarke Library Fund go to Forbes Library. A special cataloguer of the New York State Library, Beulah Bailey, was hired for three months to tackle the Clarke collection of 41,869 books and to sort out the non-duplicates of which she located more than 10,000.

In 1917, the long-needed two-story steel stack system was installed on the main floor. A 1912 engineering study had already determined that the building could indeed safely accommodate the 125,000 ton stacks with their six miles of shelving that would increase the library's capacity from 125,000 to 400,000 volumes. At this time electricity was introduced into the building via a 500-pound underground lead cable. The library was closed during all this construction that also necessitated a complete inventory and re-shelving of the collection. This same year, 1917, Librarian Harrison also vigorously supported the American Library Association's efforts to provide books and phonograph records for servicemen, following this country's entry into the First World War. At this time, Harrison also established an extensive file to record all servicemen and women from Hampshire County.

Special cataloguer Beulah Bailey of the New York State Library, was hired by the Forbes for three months to catalog the Clarke Collection of 41,869 books.

A particular contribution by Harrison was his establishment of the library's special collections; the first of which he located in the Trustees' Room, re-named the Kingsley Room after Elbridge

An American Library Association Post-Conference trip. Forbes Library, June 29, 1931.

Kingsley, a prominent Hadley artist, a number of whose works graced the library. Here, Harrison gathered the personal library of Judge Forbes, rare books designated "rb", and the Kingsley collection itself that includes books by local authors, plus local imprints and works dealing with local history. The glory of the collection is, of course, the Judd Manuscript, seventy-five volumes in all, compiled by Sylvester Judd (1789-1860) onetime editor of the *Gazette*, and, as William Cutter described him, "the final authority on matters of local history, genealogy, manners, customs, and Connecticut Valley topography ... the wonder of all authorities on local history."

Forbes Librarian Joseph LeRoy Harrison, seated at left, with his staff in 1917.

With Calvin Coolidge of Northampton serving as vice President and then as President of the United States between 1920 and 1929, Librarian Harrison wisely set to work collecting official papers, photos, scrapbooks and a variety of Coolidge memorabilia that were to form the basis of the Coolidge Collection, or nucleus of the future Calvin Coolidge Memorial Room, — the only so-called "presidential library" in the country under the

Gazette, by local historian Charles Dean, that covers the years 1786-1937.

During the Second World War, 1941-1945, Harrison marshaled Northampton's support of the

Depression-era children line up for a Christmas "Doll Reception" at the Forbes, circa 1936.

roof of a public library.

Rather than dull and grim, the years of the great depression were exciting ones in the history of the Library. Like other libraries all over the country, the Forbes experienced record-breaking levels of circulation and attendance at special events as people sought information, recreation, comfort and distraction — all of it free. Through new government agencies such as the Civil Works Administration and the Works Progress Administration, major repairs were made to the roof, the building's interior was redecorated, and a major exterior drainage system was constructed. One interesting WPA project involved the dusting of every book on the library's eleven miles of shelving — this by women. The most valuable and enduring clerical project funded by the WPA was the *Index to Local News in the Hampshire*

Victory Book Campaign to supply military libraries and once again instituted the collection of information — including a vast card file and complementary scrapbooks — on all Hampshire County servicemen and women.

During the war, on the night of March 26, 1942, fire — attributed finally to spontaneous combustion — broke out on the library's second floor. Responding to the double fire alarm at 5:25 p.m., the Northampton Fire Department had the blaze out by 6:20 p.m. Damage was confined primarily to books from the personal library of Judge Forbes. The insurance money received more than paid for salvaging and rebinding these volumes.

On a hot, humid and stifling day, July 4, 1944, an "open house" was led to celebrate the Forbes Library's fiftieth birthday. Attendance, because of the war and the weather, was sparse. In his report to the trustees that year, Harrison included a brief history of the library that, after the war, was published as a book with the title, *Forbes Library: The Half Century, 1894-1944*, with a sketch of Charles Edward Forbes.

Harrison would remain as the nominal librarian of the Forbes until his death in 1950. The last few years, however, he was not actually on the premises. So vigorous was he in his seventies when the Massachusetts Retirement System went into effect, he had chosen — unfortunately as it turned out — to remain outside the system and to continue working. In his mid-eighties, however, his health declined and his last years were spent in a nursing home. Aware that his illness had exhausted his financial resources, the library trustees generously permitted the old librarian to retain his position. Through Agnes MacGregor Collis, a secretary and order clerk, who visited him daily, Harrison maintained his contact with the library almost up to his death. A touching last gesture on the part of this old man, who had given so much of his life to the library, was his bequest of a large sum of money from his life savings that in reality no longer existed.

Coinciding dramatically — and most fortuitously — with the dynamic post-WWII era, was the librarianship of Lawrence Einar Wikander who, in 1950, came to the Forbes from Temple

University where he was Assistant Librarian, Supervisor of Technical Processes, and Acquisitions Librarian. Fresh from four years of military service, three of them spent overseas, Wikander was

On the night of March 26, 1942, fire broke out on the library's second floor. The damage was confined primarily to books from the personal collection of Judge Forbes.

young, vigorous, forward-looking and also experienced: the right man in the right place at the right time. To him fell the monumental task of reshaping the Forbes Library and redefining its mission as it moved into the second half of the twentieth century.

With that wry mixture of wit and

Lawrence E. Wikander came to the Forbes as its Librarian fresh from four years of military service. To him fell the monumental task of reshaping the library and redefining its mission as it moved into the second half of the twentieth century. Here he is returning from a library conference in Pittsburgh, PA. He is wearing his WWII combat boots. Wikander often rode his motorcycle to meetings, once going as far as Ohio.

wisdom that always graced his discourse, Wikander recorded his first impression of the physical plant: "A sense of congestion was everywhere." Procedures with

In 1953, the Forbes purchased a secondhand bookmobile to provide more and better service to new surburban housing developments. This practice ended only when Title II of the Elementary and Secondary Education Act of 1965 provided money to establish school libraries.

long-forgotten origins were still firmly in place, he discovered. "New ways were not rejected; they weren't thought of." Moving out into the community he found himself "regarded with curiosity as one who had taken vows, especially of poverty, and had withdrawn from the world." Northamptonians, he perceived, knew they had "the largest library of any town of similar size in the United States." But he also sensed that the library was somewhat remote from "the general public, the taxpayer and the businessman."

Even as he tackled the mammoth twin tasks of "house cleaning" the old building and "weeding" the collection — if such domestic terms can be applied to a library — Wikander also applied himself to internal reorganization involving staff hours, vacations and general working conditions. He also perceived the changing role of the public library and labored to make both the Forbes and himself a vital part of the community during the great national prosperity boom that followed the war. For one thing, people's life-styles had altered. Suburban living, based on the automobile, created a special challenge for the library.

In 1950, Wikander discovered, 77,074 books were drawn from the adult collection of the main library and 23,906 from the children's room. A decade later, through his promotion efforts — plus the establishment of school book-stations — main library adult circulation had risen 50% to 107,745 while the children's had doubled. At the branches and stations in suburban areas, however, children's circulation had increased by 900 %! Thus, in 1953, a secondhand bookmobile was purchased and refurbished to provide more and better service to the scattered suburban housing developments around Northampton. This function ended when Title II of the Elementary and Secondary Education Act of 1965 provided money to establish libraries in the schools themselves.

Having begun his community outreach with a talk to the South Street School PTA during Children's Book Week not long after his arrival in Northampton, Wikander soon found himself in demand by service groups throughout the area. Service on the boards and in various offices of such groups, including Rotary, proved to be the foundation of his efforts "to make the library significant to Northampton."

One of the most important and lasting of Wikander's civic contributions would be his chairmanship of the Tercentenary History Committee for the city's tercentenary celebration in 1954. As editor of *The Northampton Book*, a collection of forty-six historical essays, written by local citizens, authors, journalists and scholars, Wikander's toil and dedication produced a book still in great demand.

Two of Wikander's most visible achievements in the library were the creation of a new and modern children's room and the Calvin Coolidge Memorial Room. The first grew out of the so-called post-war "baby boom" or soaring birth rate that was producing thousands of juvenile would-be readers. In 1955 Wikander added data to his annual report showing that, despite "movies, radio, comics and television," children's reading was at an all-time high. The old second-floor room at the Forbes was proving both inadequate in size and poorly situated so the Librarian now proposed that the "well constructed room in the west side of the basement" be converted into a new children's room.

In 1958, two new library trustees, who had campaigned on this issue, secured the attention of Mayor James Cahillane who filed an order for a special $9,500 appropriation to effect an entrance to this basement room. This was followed a year later by an additional $20,500 appropriation. Money from the Insurance Fund, derived from income from the unspent portion of the loss-payment of the 1942 fire, provided funds for furnishings, equipment as well as an overhaul of the book collection. The new children's room, opened in 1959, was named after the legendary Anna Gertrude Brewster, teacher of English at

Northampton High School from 1907 to 1940. More than a teacher, Miss Brewster proved a devoted friend and mentor to many students, - particularly those who shared her love of life and literature. She inspired some of us during our college years and even wrote to us at our military stations during WWII. One such former student, Lt. Charles Kolodzinski received a letter from her during his years as a "Kriegie", or P.O.W., at Stalag Luft III in Germany. Miss Brewster, incidentally, had become the first woman trustee of the Forbes Library in1924 when she defeated a popular physician who also sought that office. She served continuously through 1957 and from 1938 on was President of the Trustees.

The Calvin Coolidge Memorial Room resulted from the vision and efforts of Librarian Wikander, Trustee Richard Garvey, a news-paperman and the youngest trustee in the library's history, and

Anna Gertrude Brewster, the legendary and much beloved teacher of English at Northampton High School, was the Forbes Library's first woman trustee.

Representative Thomas J. O'Connor, like President Coolidge, an alumnus of Amherst College. Rather than an already proposed statue of Coolidge for the State House lawn in Boston, these men envisioned a memorial room at Forbes Library in North-ampton where Coolidge lived from 1906 to 1933 and where he died. Grace Coolidge, the President's widow, approved with enthusiasm. Librarian Harrison's early notion concerning a "Coolidge Collection" now took on larger significance. On January 19, 1955, Wikander and Garvey appeared before the Committee on State Administration in Boston. The proposed room now became a reality through Chapter 547 of the Acts and Resolves of the General Court that made $32,000 available to refurbish, equip and decorate the large second-floor room at one time the medical library and later the children's story hour room and marionette theater. Present at the dedication on September 16, 1956, were Mrs. Coolidge, her son John, his wife Florence, and their daughters Cynthia and Lydia. President Coolidge's biographer,

In 1955, Richard Garvey, the youngest trustee in Forbes Library history, together with Librarian Wikander, appeared before the Committee on State Administration in Boston to propose the establishment of the Calvin Coolidge Memorial Room.

Claude Fuess, was the main speaker. Governor Christian Herter also spoke.

Among the extensive holdings of the Calvin Coolidge Memorial Room are: the President's presidential and vice presidential papers, all on file; his original governor's papers and correspondence, and a collection of more than 3,000 photos. A special treasure is the so-called Hannay Collection, a series of twenty-four large scrapbooks containing newspaper articles and feature stories, political cartoons and photos, concerning Coolidge, from newspapers and magazines, dating from 1923-1933 thus covering his vice-presidential and presidential years. Before her death, Mrs. Coolidge contributed items of family memorabilia and ephemera, now on display, as well as her own extensive correspondence. In 1992, edited by Laurence E. Wikander and Robert H. Ferrell, there was published her charming *Grace Coolidge: An Autobiography.*

Space prohibits a total listing of all of Wikander's achievements, but it should be noted that in 1962, as president of the Massachusetts Library Association, he was instrumental in founding the Western Regional Public Library System. In 1967, available state fund-

Present at the dedication of the Calvin Coolidge Room on September 16, 1956, were the president's widow, Grace Coolidge, son John with his wife, Florence, and their daughters Cynthia and Lydia.

ing made possible a regular library service, or "outreach," for patrons unable to come to the library itself. Circulation Librarian Eleanor Shea organized this service beginning with prisoners at the Hampshire County Jail and then extending it to Northampton's three elder-housing projects. Two other visible legacies of Wikander's tenure were the installation of the Art and Music Department on the second floor, in the room vacated by the children's department, and also the introduction of photo-charging on film, at the loan desk, that replaced the old "tombstone" system involving name-cards and book-card pockets.

Oliver R. Hayes succeeded Lawrence Wikander as Forbes Librarian in 1968. A graduate of Harvard and of the Columbia University School of Library Science, Hayes declared his aim of "developing the library as an instrument for fulfilling the community's needs for programs of action."

Forbes Circulation Librarian Eleanor Shea organized an "outreach" program for patrons unable to come to the library. Beginning with prisoners at the Hampshire County Jail in 1967, the service expanded to include the city's three elder-housing projects and other housebound readers living alone.

In 1968, Wikander resigned from the Forbes to accept an appointment as Librarian of Williams

College, his alma mater. As this book was being written, he confided, "My career at the Forbes Library was the most productive and enjoyable period of my life."

Wikander was succeeded by Oliver Ray Hayes, a graduate of Harvard and of the Columbia University School of Library Science, who came to the Forbes from his position as Librarian of Champlain College. Dedicated to his concept of the library as a communication center dependent on audio-visual equipment, Hayes also declared his aim of "developing the library as an instrument for fulfilling the community's need for programs of action." During his five-year stay, Hayes developed a Media Center in the belief he was moving the library "into the twentieth century." In 1973 he left to become library director at

In 1977, Stanley Greenberg was selected from a list of 70 applicants to become the Forbes library's first Director. Before his first year was complete, however, Greenberg was forced to resign due to health problems.

Eastern States Connecticut College in Willimantic, Connecticut.

Hayes' successor was James Frederic Hazel who came to the Forbes in 1974 from the Copiague Memorial Library, Copiague, N.Y. A graduate of the University of Pennsylvania, with a master's degree in library science from Drexel Institute of Technology, Hazel's stay at the Forbes was a brief three years during which he focused his attention on the Media Center. He resigned in 1977.

In November of 1977, Stanley Greenberg, who had come to the Forbes in 1962 as Reference Librarian, was selected from a list of seventy applicants to succeed Hazel as Director — the new title having replaced that of Librarian. Greenberg was well acquainted with both the library and his new role, having served as assistant librarian, as well as reference

librarian, under his three predecessors. Born in New York City, Greenberg had come as a boy to Northampton where he attended the local schools. During WWII he was seriously wounded, as a medical corpsman, with the Fifth Infantry Division in Normandy in August of 1944. After a lengthy convalescence, he earned his B.A. at Columbia University followed with an M.A. from Columbia Teachers College. After acquiring his M.L.Sc. from Simmons College, Greenberg then worked at both the Holyoke and Springfield libraries.

As Reference Librarian at the Forbes between 1962 and 1977, when he assumed the job of Director, Greenberg was noted for his tireless devotion to all patrons with their questions ranging from the frivolous to those involving the most serious professional scholarship. One such patron of the former type wanted to know how to rid his house of bats.

Upon his appointment as Director, a symbolic first project was Greenberg's effort to restore the director's office as nearly as possible to its original appearance when Charles Cutter took over as the first librarian in 1894. Down from the attic came Mr. Cutter's rocking chair and brass desk lamp; up from the cellar came his frosted-glass lampshades to be reattached to the original gas chandelier long-since converted to electricity. Greenberg's special interest in local history and genealogy led at this time to his dream — not yet realized — of a special room and staff at the library to deal specifically with Northampton history.

Before his first year as Director was completed, however, Greenberg's health problems led to his resignation. In a move inspired by both wisdom and generosity, he now recommended that his replacement be youthful Blaise Bisaillon, age thirty five, a native of Northampton, who had been the second choice of the trustees at the time of Greenberg's appointment. Bisaillon had at that time accepted the job of reference librarian and assistant director. "In effect," said Greenberg, "we simply exchanged jobs." Thus he reverted to his accustomed role which he performed until his retirement in 1982. Greenberg's daughter Carolyn, incidentally, followed in her father's footsteps, earning her M.L.Sc. at Simmons, and then securing an appointment as reference librarian and head of automation at the Lincoln Labs of the Massachusetts Institute of Technology.

Reflecting on his twenty years at the Forbes, Stanley Greenberg paused and then said: I loved the old building, I loved the collections, and I loved the people and patrons I worked with at the Forbes." His successor, Blaise Bisaillon, now took over, and thus began another new era in the history of the library.

Chapter Seven

The Elements of a Library:
Building - Collection - Staff - Money

"Don't take it! You'll regret it. You don't know what you're getting into. Go out to the midwest — or the west — where they do things right." Such was the response of his onetime supervisor in the Springfield library system to 35-year-old Blaise Bisaillon when the latter confided he had just been offered the job as Director of the Forbes Library in Northampton.

"I was stunned," says Bisaillon. "I had expected to be congratulated on my good fortune and could hardly believe what I was hearing. For a moment I thought the man was joking. The Forbes Library is a great library, and I considered my selection an honor. I realized the decision was mine alone, and I made it. And I've never regretted it."

The first native of Northampton

Forbes Library's director since 1977, Blaise Bisaillon is a Northampton native who remembers the day his father first took him to the library as a young child, and the book he chose: "A large, thin picture-book all about insects at work and at war with each other."

to head the Forbes Library, Bisaillon's experience with the institution began on the day that his father, a fireman, introduced him to the children's room then up on the second floor. "I was about six years old, I think. We walked to the Forbes from our home at 15 Summer Street. I remember the strange echo that rippled from the vaulted ceiling as our feet hit the rubber mat covering the terra cotta floor just inside the entrance. Like all other children of Northampton, I would learn how to create that echo with surreptitious stamping of my feet on the mat." Bisaillon remembers the book his father drew for him that day — "a large thin picture-book all about insects at work and at war with each other. I was particularly impressed by a picture of a huge bumblebee with one leg in a cast. I loved that book and wish I had a copy of it today."

Despite all the attractions competing for children's attention in the 1950s, the Library played a vital role in the life of young Bisaillon and his friends. "We made regular trips up the hill from Hawley Grammar School where I attended the first three grades. Then, after we moved to Bay State, my friends and I would often race off on our bikes, along the Mill River path, to the library. As a teenager, I devoured every issue of *Mad Magazine* along with books and periodicals involving cars, fishing and baseball. When I earned my B.A. and M.A. in American History at UMass, I did ninety percent of my work in the Forbes Library. I grew up in this library, but I never imagined that one day I would be its Director. I have come full circle."

Coinciding with Bisaillon's appointment in 1977 was the advent of those vast forces of change and challenge that today affect all public libraries: the so-called "information explosion", or computerization of knowledge, and, at the same time, ever-shrinking budgets caused by reduced public funding and cutbacks in federal and state aid. The Forbes

Library, because of its origins and its age, would also present problems peculiar to itself.

Every library director knows that his work involves four main components: a building, a collection, a staff and money. "Built for the ages" is how Bisaillon views the great grey granite bastion over which he presides. Constructed of steel, stone and oak according to 19th-century architectural ideals, and twice as large as libraries built in other cities the size of Northampton, the century-old Forbes Library building is at once a joy and a trial. "On a bright June morning, it is a handsome thing," says Bisaillon, "truly an aesthetic vision. The glory of this vision can fade, however, when you have to cope with crises stemming from lack of funds for proper maintenance." Such a crisis occurred during a night in March of the library's centennial year when large blocks of granite loosened and fell from the facade following a winter-long build-up of ice. A complete repointing of the building's mortar was voted by the City Council several years ago but has never been done since the deal was made contingent upon matching state funds that have been delayed five years, during which time the city's financial reserves for capital improvement have been exhausted.

On taking over as Director, one of Bisaillon's first concerns was his survey of the library's collection of some 300,000 books — about twice as many as in the libraries of other towns the size of Northampton. Scattered throughout this collection were "thousands of rare and valuable books and journals ... extraordinarily unusual: but in many instances inappropriate for a public library." Also he discovered many "prints, photographs, paintings, manuscripts and fine furniture ... equally valuable and unusual, and in the case of a few items also inappropriate for a public library." There was "no source of income for their security, restoration, repair, preservation and proper storage." Much of this hoard was in poor condition; deterioration loomed as its fate.

Together with the library trustees, Bisaillon proposed the sale of certain carefully selected books and other items to libraries, educational institutions or museums with existing collections into which these offerings would fit and thus be utilized and preserved. The sale of a Hadley Chest in 1980, for example, permitted the founding of the Special Collections Fund, the income from which today permits the preservation of photos, pictures and manuscripts of local significance and thus an integral part of the Forbes Collection.

Through the sale, in 1981, of some 30 volumes from among the many purchased by Charles Cutter at the turn of the century — books no longer used and some indeed never used — there was founded the Charles A. Cutter Book Fund, the income from which now equals that of the Book Fund established 100 years ago by Judge Forbes in his will.

The establishment of these two funds constituted milestones in the history of the library which for many years had served as a storehouse for neglected and deteriorat-

Barbara Lewis (left) and Michaela Cahillane check out books. Most visible to the library's patrons, and sometimes jokingly referred to as the "firing line," the Forbes circulation desk is where the staff handle well over 100 transactions per hour on an average day.

ing items not properly a part of its mission.

Buildings and collections alone do not constitute a library. The quality of service provided to the public depends upon the trustees and staff, and, in this connection, the Forbes Library — with a few exceptions — has always been blessed. "A constructive, supportive group of trustees is vital, and we have this under the devoted leadership of Russell Carrier," says Bisaillon. Currently there are 19 full-time and 22 part-time employees. Nine of the former hold the Master of Library Science degree while others have earned bachelor's and master's degrees in various fields of knowledge.

"We have a remarkable staff at the Forbes," says Bisaillon. "To me their most endearing and valuable attribute is their dedication to their various jobs, their pride in their work, their self respect, and the resultant respect they have for each other. They may sometimes disagree with each other about strategies, but they are united in their commitment to this library. Also fortunate here is the absence of two types, both destructive to group morale, 'slackers' and 'careerists' devoted only to themselves. The salaries at the Forbes are generally lower than in most libraries. The average annual salary for a library department head in the United States, for example, is more than $33,000. Ours at the Forbes receive about 15 percent less."

Most visible to patrons are those employees who staff the circulation desk, or loan desk, just inside the front entrance. "Patrons need to feel welcomed by the people they meet here," says Librarian Carol Murphy, head of the Circulation Department, "so we try to be welcoming." Sometimes jokingly referred to as the "firing line," the circulation desk used to handle about 70 transactions per hour. The all-day Thursday, plus evening and Sunday afternoon closings, have increased this number to well over 100 per hour.

"People are indeed still reading," says Murphy. "Last year our circulation here at the main desk alone reached 123,134, and we have about 400 titles on reserve at all times. We are still dealing with the effects of our recently computerized system which, although admittedly efficient, nevertheless takes more time. Also, we lose some of the eye contact and easy give-and-take with patrons — both of which we miss." Murphy has two permanent full-time assistants, William Kenefick and Susan Montague, and one permanent part-time assistant, Claire Fournier. Regular part-timers on the desk are Charlotte Leighton, who supplies the flowers that grace the desk year round, Moira Callahan, Barbara Lewis, and Patricia McLain. Six additional part-timers enable coverage of the desk at all times the library is open: Emily Bisbee, Michaela Cahillane, Adam Goss, Daniel Jarvis, Robert Noble and Kim Perez.

Nearby on the main floor, is the Reference Department presided over by Reference Librarian Elise Bernier-Feeley and her part-time assistant, Elise Dennis. "People look on the reference librarian as an oracle, " says Feeley. "Every question is important to us. We love research, and we love people. We don't know everything, but we do know how to locate information that is wanted." She remembers working on her M.L.S. thesis here at the Forbes and occasionally glancing up at the portrait of Charles Cutter. To herself she would say: "Someday, Mr. Cutter, I would like to work in your library."

Examples of the inquiries that day are: tourist information on Switzerland; the Hampshire County jail; the Stebbins family genealogy; New Orleans cuisine; Connecticut Valley cabinet-makers; estrogen therapy; electric food-steamers; testing for AIDS; new car guides; comic-book collecting; information on area preparatory schools; sources of career information; the fall and winter census for 1850; the history of the Florence Congregational Church. The last question of the day: "Are there any polo clubs in New England?"

Helping a patron with some research questions is Head Reference Librarian Elise Bernier-Feeley (left), who presides over the Forbes' Reference Room with Reference Librarian Elise "Tibby" Dennis. Between them, they field one-third of the library's service requests.

On a summer day in 1993, between 8:30 a.m. and 5:30 p.m. Feeley was observed fielding questions directed at her by 64 patrons in the reference room — some of whom also required instruction in the use of the technical equipment there. An additional 34 inquiries during the day reached her by telephone — some to be dealt with immediately while others had to go on the answering-machine to be answered later.

At the close of the day, a half cup of coffee and a partially eaten doughnut still sat where Feeley had placed them that morning and never got to finish. "Not a bad day, actually," she observed, "although it was busier than usual because of yesterday's Thursday closing. There's work enough here for three reference librarians. This is a very special community — so many educated and energetic people always in search of information."

The Reading Room, also on the main floor, is the responsibility of Maureen Barron who, as a member of the Technical Services or Catalog Department does the purchasing, billing and renewals of all the newspapers and periodicals made available to readers. "We provide 12 different newspapers and more than three hundred periodicals for our patrons," says Barron, "and you can't imagine what a tangle those newspapers are in at the end of a busy day."

Barron arrives at 7 each morning to pick up, sort out and re-shelve, in proper order, all the publications left scattered about from the previous day. She adds the latest newspaper to the stacks that are culled of old papers at the end of each week. These go to files in the basement.

"We have a steady flow of patrons," says Barron, "some of them quite regular such as the man who comes in each day to read *The Wall Street Journal.* One of the most unusual events in this room was the wedding in 1993 of one of our staff, Mary Bracchi Ragan."

At the rear of the library, on the main floor, is the Business and Acquisitions Department headed by Ellen Dugal. "Everything begins here, and everything ends here," says this 33-year veteran of the Forbes who worked there as a page during her years at Northampton High School. Her assistant, Nancy Graham, also worked as a page while a student at St. Michael's High School.

"It's unusual to have the business and acquisitions functions combined as we do here," says Dugal. "Most libraries have two offices to do what we believe we do more efficiently in one. Nancy is responsible for acquisitions while I monitor and manage the library's finances including the twice-monthly payroll, preparing the warrants for the payment of bills that go to the trustees for approval, and then paying the bills."

"We also handle the library's various funds including Judge Forbes Aid Fund that goes toward such things as supplies and utilities; the Watson Fund used for items we don't ask the city for, — such as computers, office renovations and other special projects; the Cutter Fund; and the Judge Forbes Book Fund which has relieved the city of ever having to buy a book for the library. In this last case, we prepare an annual book expenditure report so that the trustees and our department heads know what we have to spend."

"Our problems are time and money," Dugal concludes. "Never enough of either to do what needs to be done. There is a severe parking problem, for example, and our collection, computers and copiers all suffer from the lack of climate control. I'm proud that we make the best use of every dollar that we do have, and I know that the Forbes Library is the biggest bargain in Northampton."

Down on the basement level is the Technical Services Department head by Librarian Alexce Douville — who serves as automation librarian and cataloguer. She is assisted by Kathryn Mizula, Joanne Petcen and two part-time employees, Paula Elliot and Portia Henle. "We receive and catalog each item that comes into the library," says Douville, "every book, periodical, musical score, whatever. Each new item is given a classification number that goes into the data base, and we are, incidentally, the only library using Charles Cutter's system. Most public libraries use the Dewey Decimal System, while academic libraries use the Library of Congress System that is based on Cutter's. Upon release each new

98

item goes to William Kenefick in Circulation who checks to see if it is on request and, if not, it goes on the shelf."

Because of her technical expertise, Douville was added to the staff when the Forbes prepared to join the Central Western Massachusetts Automation Resource Sharing network known informally as C/W MARS. "We have put 132,000 records into the system; there are still about 130,000 to be added — mostly older items from the Kingsley Collection for example. Our plans for the future," says Douville, "involve a computerized access catalog that will permit patrons to search our data base using a single key word not just the old author, subject and title approach. About 60 libraries in Western Massachusetts — both public and academic — already have this. It will cost about $36,000, and we are seeking funding."

As to the future of books, Douville observes: "There are always going to be books. No one wants to take a mirofiche or a computer to bed along with their popcorn. I know I don't."

The Anna Gertrude Brewster Children's Room, named after the Northampton High School's legendary teacher of English and the library's first woman trustee, is also on the basement level. Headed by Librarian Jude Kingsbury, the children's librarian, this department — following its recent extensive renovation — has proved a magnet for children and their parents. Kingsbury, who is assisted by Mary Ragan and Sandra Jodie, says, "We wanted this to be a place where children's faces light up, and it is. They come here from the time they are

The recently renovated Anna Gertrude Brewster Children's Room on the basement level of the library has proved a magnet for local children and their parents, including these three young readers acting out a story with Children's Librarian Jude Kingsbury.

If it's Friday, it's book day at the Walter Salvo House. Charles Maiewski and Robert Montague, who run Forbes Library's Outreach Department, help residents select books during one of their weekly visits to the elder housing project on Conz Street. The dining area includes a mini-library and sign-out desk for residents who gather on the arrival of "Charlie" and "Bob" as they are known there.

able to toddle through the doorway until they are 13 to 14. We cater to the various ages in our Picture Book Room for the youngest, the Easy Reader Room for those in the early grades, the Fiction Area for older kids, and the Young Adult Area for the early teens. We have a constant series of special features that include storytime, films, contests, and in summer a weekly 'brown-bag' lunch with a storyteller."

At mid-morning on a July day in 1993 there were 18 children in the room — plus two parents and a nanny — all of them studying the shelves and making selections. Then entered a group of eight involved in a summer reading project dealing with other countries. A young father, with a day off, came in with his three sons aged four, six and eight. "We're here for our bedtime books. They don't want to go to sleep until we've read to them which we've done since they were born."

Some children are brought in

with their day-care group. "One of our favorite groups comes from the People's Institute," says Kingsbury. "They are lively kids and enjoy their visit, but they are proud to demonstrate what their young leader refers to as their 'library manners.'"

"In a society filled with a wide variety of commercial distractions competing for children's attention," says Kingsbury, "we are trying to get them into books." Apparently they are succeeding in light of the 1993 circulation figure of 105,448. "And with the current recession, our number of users," she adds, "keeps going up."

Headed by Charles Maiewski, assisted by Robert Montague, the Outreach Department, that carries books on a weekly basis to people who cannot come to the library, is also quartered on the basement level. Their patrons include people living in elder-housing complexes, housing projects, and nursing homes. At the Walter Salvo house, a mini-library and sign-out desk are set up for residents who gather on the arrival of "Charlie" or "Bob" as they are known.

"Many of the people you'll visit are lonely," advised Eleanor Shea, the onetime circulation librarian who developed Outreach in 1966 and who trained Maiewski and Montague. "Don't rush off. Give them a few minutes if they seem to need this. You're doing more than deliver books. You are their contact with the community." This philosophy still guides Outreach today.

Some readers submit specific book requests; some indicate various fields of interest; others rely on the two men to choose books for them. "I don't always read every book you bring me," confided one of the latter. "That's okay," was the response. "We don't give quizzes." Another reader enjoys savoring new ideas in the books chosen for him by someone else.

"They are wonderful, these two gentlemen," says one elderly reader. "I have to read all night long, and the books they bring me from the Forbes are a great comfort." Another regular recipient says, "Life would be much more difficult for me without the Forbes. The library is a haven for people like me even though it has to come to us."

The Art and Music Department up on the library's second floor is headed by librarian Faith Kaufman assisted full-time by Brian Tabor and part-time by Sallie Pitt. They provide a wide range of services to the public through an extensive collection of art books — approximately 16,750 — as well as periodicals in this field. Music books and scores, numbering some 4,000, include

many that are old and unavailable elsewhere and thus of special use to area musicians.

The Art and Music Department circulates about 2,000 compact disks and 2,000 cassettes, with 1,500 of the latter in music and the rest books on tape. These disks and cassettes boast the heaviest circulation of the library. Almost half of this collection is out at any given time, and each item circulates 10 to 11 times a year for two-week loan periods, or about 10 times the rate for books. To this collection are added about 600 titles each year that include classical, jazz, rock, theater, film and folk disks. Records are no longer purchased, but the department's 4,500 records still circulate.

The department also oversees the library's renowned collections of photographs, prints, paintings and posters. A special contribution by the department consists of regularly scheduled monthly exhibits by local artists and photographers, the bookings for which have to be made a year in advance so great is the demand for space. Concerts funded by the Friends of the Forbes Library or the Northampton Arts Council range from chamber music and classical guitar to jazz and bluegrass.

Except for the frustration she experiences at the unavailability of funds to properly care for the collection and the historic building, Kaufman finds joy in her work at the Forbes. "Northampton is a very special place. I like this community and especially that segment of it that uses the library — interesting, intelligent, nice people. We have a wonderful art and music collection, and they make good use of it. Many are artists or musicians themselves. This library is perfect for Northampton and also for me." Somewhat shyly she added: "There is another wonderful thing about the Forbes. The staff here is like a family."

Open on a part-time basis, due to lack of funding, is the second-floor Calvin Coolidge Memorial Room in the care of Archivist Lu Knox. The presidential, vice-presidential and gubernatorial papers are all on microfilm, but there are thousands of original documents, photographs and political cartoons, plus the Hannay Scrapbook of newspaper and magazine clippings that record the Coolidge presidency — all in need of preservation work and climate control. "The Calvin Coolidge collection," says Knox, "contains primary source materials not available in any other collection in the world."

Knox's duties include assisting researchers filling requests for photos and research materials, greeting visitors and preparing special exhibits such as the 1993-94 exhibit entitled *Grace Coolidge: First Lady of Northampton.* This exhibit was mounted in connection with the publication of *Grace Coolidge An Autobiography* edited by Lawrence Wikander.

The one department upon which all others in the library depend is that managed by Head Custodian Donald Finn and known as Maintenance. Michael Burke and Jason Myers, each working half time, are his assistants. Myers is about to assume this role full-time alone.

"I take care of this old place," says Finn on being asked his duties. "Actually, I took on this job as a fluke in 1972 after working

Maintenance of the 100-year-old Forbes Library building is in the capable hands of Head Custodian Donald Finn and his assistants Michael Burke and Jason Myers. Here, Finn — who has a number of strings to his bow, including computer know-how — lends Susan Montague a hand with a problem at her desk.

seven years on the circulation desk. I enjoy what I do and take a real interest in it and have never looked back. I love this old building and probably know more about it now than anyone else. I see that all the routine maintenance work gets done, but I also see what needs to be done for this

100-year-old building and make recommendations. I feel almost personally the neglect of basic repairs like those needed on the second-floor window frames, not to mention the masonry."

Finn can turn his hand to almost anything, and he has. In between his never-ending battles with grass, leaves and snow, he repairs gutters up on the roof, installs shelving in the children's room, and does plaster repair and painting. "The director and the trustees learned that I have some talents that are needed around here," says Finn, "and they use them." He is credited by the Business and Acquisitions Department by aiding them in finding an IBM compatible computer, with more programs, and costing $1,000 less than others under consideration. He is particularly proud of his role in the creation of the new Technical Services work area. It was he who proposed and carried out the transformation of a forbidding onetime coal-bin area in the basement into a much-needed attractive and functional work area. "I saw the potential," he says, "and did much of the work myself including putting up the walls, installing the doors, and painting. The work I couldn't do, we hired out. That room came into being for about $6,000 or one fourth of what it could have cost. I also did the lobby for the new children's room."

"My department," says Finn with pride, "is the only one that doesn't cost money. We seldom ask for anything. Instead, we provide savings for the library."

The fourth component in the operation of a library is money. Northamptonians have always

been proud of the fact that their city has long enjoyed the services of the largest and best library of any city of its size in the nation.

Because of Judge Forbes' Book Fund, and subsequent gifts to the library, the city has never had to buy any of the hundreds of thousands of books available to patrons over the last 100 years. Agreed to when it accepted Judge Forbes' gift, the city's responsibility has been to pay the employees' salaries and to maintain the building. Due to Judge Forbes' Aid Fund, and other gifts, the city's burden has always been substantially lessened. The Commonwealth of Massachusetts, morever, recognizing that the Forbes provides services beyond the city limits of Northampton, has therefore been making a sizable annual grant to the Forbes.

Due to these private funds, plus state assistance, the City of Northampton has been able to "buy" the Forbes Library's extensive services for each citizen of this city at less than eight cents a day. This has meant that the city could meet the commitment it made, on accepting Judge Forbes' gift, for less than two percent of its annual budget. In this time of recession when all Massachusetts cities and towns are facing severe budget restraints, even this modest contribution to the Forbes has been constricted. The *Gazette's* headline back on October 24, 1894, the day following the library's dedication, now seems both prophetic and ironic: "Forbes Library. It Is Now Ours To Fight Over and Pay For."

Given the fixed services and maintenance costs for the Forbes, the only place where cuts can be made is in personnel costs and repairs on the century-old building. The long-needed repointing of the exterior masonry has not been done, and in 1992 the trustees agreed to close the library to the public every Thursday, and in addition reduce the weekly hours of service, from 63 to 49, to save $25,000 of a $49,000 reduction following the defeat of a local over-ride attempt. This last measure has caused the Commonwealth of Massachusetts to serve notice that it must sharply reduce its annual grant to the Forbes unless the latter restores its 63 hours per week of service to the public. The concomitant irony in this "no win" situation is that, during "hard times," the usage of libraries always increases.

"For the past 12 years we have been "belt-tightening,'" says Director Bisaillon. "Some good has resulted, for we are experiencing far more productivity per dollar than was true 15 years ago. We have cut away the fat and are now down to the bone. At this point, all cuts directly damage basic library service. No further economies are possible unless we reduce the payroll by locking the door to the library."

Chapter Eight

The Educational, Informational, and Cultural Center of this Community

The history of the library over the over the past 14 years includes a major policy change in 1983 when, at the instigation of trustee Russell Carrier, the terms of Judge Forbes' will were legally altered to increase the number of trustees from three to five — considered a more practical and workable arrangement — and also to permit them to appoint the secretary and treasurer for the library. The term "none but laymen" was eliminated, and an investment policy more modern and better suited to contemporary economics was instituted. This last alteration resulted, over a decade, in the tripling of the income available for book purchases, ie., from $35,000 in 1983 to $130,000 in 1993.

Another significant achievement was the founding in 1980 of the Friends of Forbes Library by Gertrude Smith, a retired Smith College professor of music. The Friends have proved friends indeed. Their contributions range from personal service and public advocacy to generous gifts of money for specific needs, identified by the library staff, such as terminals and printers for the ref-

The Forbes Staff, 1994 - the library's Centennial Year.

erence department, a 34-volume dictionary of art for the art and music department, and their annual $2,000 contribution to the book budget. Since their founding, their gifts have totaled around $200,000.

A massive book inventory, inspired and organized by Alexce Douville and her staff in 1988, consumed five days of intensive work, from 7 a.m. to 10 p.m. on the part of more than 30 members of the staff. Of the more than 150,000 books involved on the two floors of the steel stacks, 15,000 books still listed in the catalog finally had to be declared missing. Their disappearance had obviously taken place in those years before the installation in 1983 of the 3M Book-Detection System to combat annual thefts of some $30,000 worth of books and periodicals. The entire cost of the system, $17,375, was met by a $5,000 gift from the Friends, one of $1,000 from an anonymous donor, and the rest from the Watson Fund.

Two major technological advances have reached the Forbes in recent years. In 1989 the library received a federally-funded state grant to install workstations, hardware and CD-ROM projects for experimental usage in the Reference Room. At no cost to the city, InfoTrac and ProQuest are now serving library patrons. Automation of the outmoded circulation system at the Forbes began in 1991 with the installation of the C/W MARS computerized system now in operation.

The Calvin Coolidge Memorial Room, renovated and redecorated in 1983, became the recipient in 1988 of a $125,000 grant from the U.S. National Archives that permitted the original papers from Coolidge's years as Governor of Massachusetts to be organized, indexed and microfilmed together with other personal papers of President Coolidge donated by his son, John Coolidge. The entire collection of Coolidge papers, that includes the microfilmed presidential and vice-presidential papers, is now accessible via computer. The National Archives grant came about through the efforts of a one-time Northampton resident and employee at the Forbes, Michael Russell, Legislative Director for Senator Arlen Specter (PA.), and also the timely support of Representative Silvio Conte.

A welcome addition to the library's trust funds came in 1992 through the will of Elsa Jillson Nichols — a gift of $300,000 to be known as the Nichols Book Fund. This is the largest gift to the library since that of Judge Forbes a century ago.

Perhaps the major legacy of the library trustees, administration and staff in the period leading up to the library's centennial is the Library Improvement Plan that emerged from an exhaustive study begun by the Long Range Planning Committee in 1984. Four priorities, or goals, were established: handicap access to the library; a transformation of the Anna Gertrude Brewster Children's Room; the creation of the Hampshire Room to house the library's vast local-and-area history collection; a much-needed expansion and renovation of the Reference Room; and redesign of the circulation department's area.

"Our problem is not size," says Bisaillon. "It is space and the proper utilization thereof. Ideally, 50 percent of the space in a library is allotted to the collection, 30 percent to the patrons or users, and 15 to 20 percent for staff work areas.

"At the Forbes, even with our ongoing 'weeding' process, we have about 80 percent of our usable space occupied by books, 12 percent in use by our patrons, and only eight percent left for the staff to work in. Thus we have the situation where approximately one third of our library service takes place in the Reference Room that presently occupies only five percent of our space. We have to address this and other space utilization problems."

Consisting of an exterior chairlift at the entrance and a four-stop interior elevator, the proposed handicap access became a reality in 1987. The system was constructed at a cost of $165,000 — $150,000 of which came from federal sources with the remaining $15,000 acquired from private ones. The lavish new room for children, dedicated in 1992, was made possible by the sale to the Asian Studies Department at UMass of the Benjamin Smith Lyman Oriental language books that had been in storage in the basement since 1920. Supplemented by $40,000 privately raised, the sale of the unused Lyman collection provided the total $240,000 cost of this project. No public money was involved.

The next major project for the Library Improvement Plan involves the creation of the Hampshire Room to be built in 2,000 square feet of space available on the second floor where the so-called media center once func-

tioned. In terms of function and relocation, the Hampshire Room will involve the library's most extensive change in the use of space. Currently, the Forbes Library's rich hoard of local history materials is scattered in nine different areas on three different levels. United at last in one coherent collection in the Hampshire Room will be more than 12,000 books on local and area history, a superb collection of 18th and 19th-century newspapers, letters, diaries, manuscripts, maps, pamphlets, account books and thousands of 19th and early 20th-century photographs. The room will be staffed by currently employed personnel.

"The failure to establish a Hampshire Room for the purpose described constitutes the most glaring omission in the organizational development of the Forbes Library," believes Bisaillon. "We have the collection, we have the staff, and we have the demand. Without the proper facilities, our ability to provide optimal library service concerning local history is compromised or prevented every day ... we have to preserve the record of our past even as we work at preparing this great library for the 21st century."

Seated in the same chair before the same desk in the same office occupied by the legendary "Mr. Cutter" when the Forbes Library opened a century ago, Bisaillon often grows reflective. "We are passing through a trying era of transition complicated by shrinking funds. We find ourselves pressured to do more and more with less and less and — at the same time — challenged to prove the value of the library to the community. We are doing our best. We may never enjoy the fruits of our labor, but we are seeing to it that the Forbes Library will remain the educational, informational and cultural center of this community for years to come."

Judge Charles E. Forbes

Forbes Library Trustees

Photography and graphics credits

We would like to thank the following institutions and individuals who have provided, or given permission to reprint, the illustrations in this book:

Daily Hampshire Gazette

First Churches of Northampton

Forbes Library

Richard Garvey

Greenfield Historical Society

Historic Northampton

Roger Lincoln & Elizabeth Howe Lincoln (for illustration on page 29 from *Quabbin: The Lost Valley,* by Donald W. Howe)

Allison Lockwood

Smith College Archives

Smith College Museum of Art

Lawrence E. & Marie Wikander

Bibliography

Books, Manuscripts consulted:

Burt, Henry M.
Charles Edward Forbes, founder of Forbes Library, biographical sketch. Typescript.
Northampton, MA., 1897.

Cutter, William P.
Charles Ammi Cutter
Chicago, IL. American Library Association. 1931.

Dean, Charles
Charles Edward Forbes, LL.D. Founder of Forbes Library
Northampton, MA.
Typescript. 1963.

Forbes, Charles Edward
Journal, 1839-1881.
Forbes Library

Forbes Library Annual Reports
1895-1994

Harrison, Joseph L.
Forbes Library: The Half Century, 1894-1944.
Northampton: The Print Shop, 1945.

Little, Agnes E.
Charles Ammi Cutter
Univ. North Carolina. Thesis, 1962

Miksa, Francis Louis
Charles Ammi Cutter, 1837-1903
Univ. Chicago. Thesis, 1970.

Mikander, Lawrence E.
Disposed to Learn: The First Seventy-Five Years of the Forbes Library.
Northampton, MA. 1972.

Newspapers consulted:

Daily Hampshire Gazette

Hampshire County Journal

Hampshire Gazette & Northampton Courier

Northampton Daily Herald

Index

Bold type indicates photo